Social Purpose and Schooling

Dedication

To Bill and Gladys without whose
unflinching support during some dark
years all that went before this book
would have been impossible.

Social Purpose and Schooling:
Alternatives, Agendas and Issues

Jerry Paquette

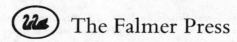 The Falmer Press

(A member of the Taylor & Francis Group)
London • New York • Philadelphia

UK   The Falmer Press, 4 John Street, London WC1N 2ET
USA   The Falmer Press, Taylor & Francis Inc., 1900 Frost Road, Suite 101, Bristol, PA 19007

First published 1991

British Library Cataloguing in Publication Data
A catalogue record of this book is available from the British Library

Library of Congress Cataloguing-in-Publication Data
Paquette, Jerald E., 1946–
    Social purpose and schooling: alternatives, agendas, and issues/
Jerry Paquette.
       p.   cm.
    Includes bibliographical references (p.   ) and index.
    ISBN 1-85000-920-1—ISBN 1-85000-921-X (pbk.):
    1. Education—Social aspects—Great Britain.   2. Education and state—Great Britain. I. Title.
LC191.8.G7P37 1991
370.19′0941—dc20   91-14735
                                                CIP

Jacket design by Caroline Archer

Typeset in 11/13 Bembo by
Graphicraft Typesetters Ltd., Hong Kong

Printed in Great Britain by Burgess Science Press, Basingstoke on paper which has a specified pH value on final paper manufacture of not less than 7.5 and is therefore 'acid free'.

Contents

List of Figures and Tables

Glossary of Terms

ASP   Assisted Places Scheme
CTC   City Technology College
DES   Department of Education and Science
HMI   Her Majesty's Inspectors
LEA   Local Education Authority
OECD Organization for Economic Cooperation and Development

Preface

Why a book on social purpose and education — and why now? The answers are simple and compelling, even if the issues themselves are elusive and complex. So much of what has been written about education, even about the sociology of education, either isolates institutionalized human learning from broader issues of social purpose, from evolving ideas of who we are and what we wish to become, or integrates education and broad social policy issues only within the context of a single ideological perspective. In a world of nations suddenly grown multicultural and technological, new questions and dilemmas crowd and confound the enduring ones of why and what we are as peoples, nations and persons. Much evidence suggests that we are at a watershed in our sense of social purpose. No longer can we cling to comforting cultural homogeneity as a pillar of stability in our collective sense of self and country. No longer does cultural and linguistic homogeneity, real or imagined, suggest the possibility of a social cohesion rooted in sameness. The perennial issues of equalizing educational opportunity and results contend today, even in technologically advanced countries, with resource scarcity and with a need for differentiated labour in an entirely new and unfamiliar context, that of the post-industrial technological revolution and an emerging 'cult of information'.[1]

In such circumstances, the isolation of educational policy issues from larger issues of social and economic purpose is fraught with danger. At the very least, the dangers include self-delusion and commitment of large sums of public monies to unrealizable goals — or unworkable processes. At worst, the isolation of educational policy from our efforts to understand and influence what we are becoming as peoples and nations, leads to a pervasive institutional mythology that belies the reality of formal education experienced by the majority of students in our schools. A large and growing literature of radical research and critique exists which turns upside down conventional ways of viewing the function and impact of education. Schools, such critics suggest, far from equalizing opportunity, serve mainly to formalize and legitimate long-term inequality, an inequality recently and greatly exacerbated by automation and the accompanying displacement of skilled labour, as well as lower, and increasingly even middle, management.

If publicly delivered education has fallen considerably short of its promise of equal opportunity for all, surely it is neither, on the one hand, a helpless victim of circumstances beyond its control nor, on the other, responsible alone for its considerable shortfalls. Schooling, institutionalized learning in the broadest sense, occurs within, in fact at the very nexus of, the strivings and conflict of diverse groups in national and regional societies to shape their particular and collective destinies. These political contests pit fatalistic determinism against faith that political process can influence significantly the evolution of societies and their cultural fabric. Much of our collective experience nudges us toward acceptance of the fatalistic social creed of logical positivism: we are powerless before social forces which inexorably determine our destiny. Yet the tenacity with which many of the major industrial nations have held to at least nominally democratic political institutions suggest we continue to dream of consciously shaping both our social purpose and the beliefs, commitments and knowledge of the young.

Central to that dream is learning — not just amassing academic knowledge, but acquiring values and commitments to live and act by. The real questions of the hour in education and social policy have to do with what we wish to become — and with the ability or inability of schooling to help us become what we wish. The utility of schooling as an instrument of social purpose hinges in part, at least, on the type of schooling arrangements we establish and allow. Inevitably, however — and whether or not we acknowledge it — these arrangements take their form from shared ideas of social purpose. We create a sort of hermeneutic cycle of social purpose and schooling in which each continually shapes the other.

Given the importance of learning to societal cohesion, survival and change, the way we understand schooling arrangements should be framed within the context of seminal views of social purpose widely shared and understood among those who shape and seek to shape public policy. Chapter 2 presents and reviews three alternative views of social purpose and their relationships with educational policy thought. Chapter 3 examines two frameworks for categorizing schooling arrangements in light of the alternative views of social purpose presented in the preceding chapter.

Societies are never static. The latter half of the twentieth century has, by any standards and precedent, however, been a period of remarkable social, economic and technological change. These changes need to be part of any analysis and evaluation of schooling efforts and how they serve and interact with social purpose. That is the mission of chapter 4.

The usefulness of a framework for understanding schooling arrangements must be measured against its ability to provide insight into both typical and unusual schooling arrangements that have evolved and appear to be evolving. Chapter 5 examines generically different schooling arrangements and their implications. Chapter 6 details recent efforts of the Tory Government to reshape schooling arrangements in Britain in ways that differ markedly from arrangements in most other industrially advanced, democratic countries. Chapter 7 juxtaposes and weighs the major claims and counterclaims of those who propose to move schooling arrangements in the direction of more or less public control, funding and regulation.

The emergence of social and structural pluralism as an important agenda of social purpose is related to the changed demography of many technologically advanced countries. Chapter 8 examines in detail the nature of, and the assumptions behind, competing claims of those who advocate more or less minority language and culture in school curricula. In reviewing the arguments and assumptions behind the educational pluralism issue, I suggest a complex interplay of that issue with the more generic issues surrounding public and private education.

Finally, in chapter 9, I review the meta-issues and conclude that we may all stand more to benefit than to lose from ongoing rethinking and restructuring of schooling arrangements — so long as these rearrangements do not erode even further whatever contribution to more equal life-chances schooling confers on pupils from diverse backgrounds.

Note

1 The origin of this suggestive term appears to be Theodore Roszak, *The Cult of Information: The Folklore of Computers and the True Art of Thinking* (New York: Pantheon, 1986).

Chapter 1

Education and Social Purpose: The Front Line of Ideology

How to find direction and set a course as societies in a maelstrom of social, economic and technical change is the central problem confronting most peoples and their governments in the latter decades of the twentieth century. In the face of vast newfound technical capabilities — and problems — a volatile combination of boundless optimism and fatalistic determinism shapes and limits discussion of fundamental issues of social purpose. A profoundly mixed reaction to the brave new world in which we live kindles both dialogue and confrontation over what we wish to become as peoples and nations. We cannot judge with certainty, of course, whether we have more or less power over our social destiny than previous generations since much of the evidence lies in history yet to be enacted. Beyond the problem of not knowing what has not yet happened, however, lies the inherent ambiguity of the word power, an ambiguity which will continue to vex the issue of how much control we really do have over our collective fate even when and if a definitive history of our era is written.

Rightly or wrongly schools are generally viewed, even by their worst critics, as important instruments of social policy. More than that, they are highly visible, and highly costly, symbols of official policy aimed at shaping who we are and become as nations and peoples. In fact, the vision of schools shared by many, if not most, stakeholders in education is strikingly reminiscent of the view Catholics and orthodox Christians have long had of their sacraments, that is, things which bring about what they symbolize. Certainly the idea that schools affect learning and shape values has not been undisputed, but the persistence of public support for all forms of schooling strongly suggests that most people believe schools are important elements affecting the knowledge, values and culture of the young — as well as their life chances.

If schools powerfully symbolize and shape knowledge and values, if they are in that respect a sort of secular, social sacrament (whatever the moral or religious content of the education they provide) — *or even if people only believe they are* — then schools unavoidably become a natural focus for all the energies of competing cultures and belief-systems seeking control of the minds and allegiance of the young. Perennial contests, struggles and battles to gain control of school curricula, and endless debate over what knowledge is of the most worth are fuelled by faith in the efficacy of schools as transmitters, however imperfect or perverse, of knowledge and culture.

Control over both the form of schooling and its academic and moral content is the symbolic battlefield whereon ideas, beliefs and cultures struggle perpetually for more control of what societies will be like in the future. Struggle for control over schooling thus becomes the ultimate public-policy crucible in which our vision of social purpose is tried. For that reason, the major ideologies vying for control over the way people think about social and economic relationships have inescapable counterparts in schooling content and arrangements.

Not long ago, the rationale for a predominately publicly-funded, operated and controlled schooling arena seemed fairly obvious. Schools were instruments of social policies aimed at economic stability and growth, and at equalizing educational opportunity and life-chances. They were needed engines of assimilation and moral indoctrination into majority cultures, languages and ethical standards. Today, all of these assumptions about the purposes of schooling are, at the very least, contested. That they are so is the result of many changes, but above all perhaps, the result of renewed debate about social purpose and about the assumptions which undergird the major agendas of social purpose in modern societies. Interest in such questions is no longer limited to academics and political ideologues. Parents and non-parents alike seem less disposed than in the past to accept uncritically the assumptions and claims which underpin monolithic state-sponsored education.

Current widespread scepticism, soul-searching and experimentation in educational and social policy is almost certainly related to profound changes in the way we live and work as well as in our cultural and linguistic make-up. Urgently needed are:

1 a framework for understanding, comparing and contrasting the driving agendas of social purpose, that is, our most generic and widely shared ideas about the good life in the best society practically possible;

2 a framework for making sense of how schooling is and can be orchestrated in different conditions and times; and

3 an exploration of potential relationships between these two frameworks.

Only with such tools can one hope to make sense of the dizzying array of arrangements for schooling which exist in various countries and regions. Only with such tools can one organize useful research into the effects of different approaches to schooling in different contexts. What follows is an attempt to lay the foundations for a workable and useful way of making sense of the burgeoning diversity in schooling arrangements across the world, and, perhaps more importantly, to link different approaches to schooling to different ideas about social purpose. Finally, none of this will be very useful to anyone unless such frameworks and linkages take into account the enormous social, cultural, life-style and work-style changes which confront and challenge each of us in almost every aspect of our daily lives. Completing the circle of social and educational policy, then, requires major attention to change and to the issues it raises, and that examination of change is the final, major agenda of this book, and the main business of chapters 3 and 8.

Chapter 2

Ideologies and the Agenda of Schooling

What are the central agendas of social purpose which contend for the power to shape our society? What are their counterparts in educational purpose? What alternatives do these agendas suggest in how we sponsor, organize and judge learning? Finally, what issues do these alternatives raise for our schools and for the society which creates, legitimates and empowers them?

We live in a world in which people hold fundamentally different visions of what human societies ought to accomplish for their members (as well as of what they do in fact accomplish). Proponents of differing perspectives vie for acceptance of their particular vision and for the power to direct social policy according to the assumptions behind that vision. In the end, we can neither solve nor ignore the dilemma of social function. In an existence increasingly choreographed by large, private and public organizations, we need — perhaps desperately — to know what such organizations do both for us and to us. Yet, an apparently intractable irony of the human condition is that, in the absence of agreement about some 'right' model of human organizations and human society generally, we cannot reach consensus about the effects of organizations and policies. Even as we hone, diversify and redouble research efforts to evaluate the impacts of organizations and of public social policy, we are condemned (or perhaps privileged, if we value diversity) to fundamental and ongoing disagreement about what our institutions do to and for people. This inevitable disagreement follows directly from the differing values and assumptions which underpin alternative models of human organizations and society.

Our assumptions about social reality shape the questions we ask about it. Those who consider human society a battleground among contending interest groups pitted against one another in the social equivalent of gladiatorial combat, will ask questions very different, for instance, from the questions asked by those who think of human society as a well-oiled machine. Moreover, beyond, in the first place, limiting the scope of inquiry into human institutions, beliefs about the nature of human society inevitably shape the interpretation of data in social inquiry.

In the end, research data never speak for themselves. They must always be interpreted and we have only our own preferred model of human society, and the values and beliefs behind our model, to shape that interpretation. What the data produced by a study of social or educational policy or practice *means* will ultimately depend on beliefs and assumptions used in their interpretation — and hence *the same data will mean many things to many people.* In educational as in sociological research generally, the tradition of 'reinterpreting' a researcher's results with different assumptions is now well established. Only the naive now believe that research can lead to clarity, certainty and consensus about the effects on people of institutions and social policies.

Not being able to prove the correctness of one's favourite interpretation of social reality to proponents of competing views, however, rarely inhibits either fervour of belief or willingness to prescribe public policy on the basis of that belief. Those who believe society is like a machine remain committed to remedying social problems through 'structural change', while those who view society as a battlefield of the classes, are quick to suggest stratagems for winning the battle. *How our institutional arrangements, as such, affect people is ultimately unknowable.* Indeed, such arrangements may not exist at all in any meaningful way apart from the action and beliefs of persons who work in and are touched by them.

My purpose here, however, is not to discuss the effects of human institutions and how we can come to know these effects. Neither is it to minimize the importance of working to understand how people affect other people in institutions and in society at large. Rather I want to stake out clearly the scope of the discussion that follows, which has to do with value commitments that lead to agendas of social purpose that in turn lead to particular approaches to public policy, including educational policy. Convictions about the nature of human society and human institutions shape how we understand them and how we inquire into the action of persons within them. The same convictions shape our prescriptions for what society *ought to do* for its various members, and how it can best do this.

Coherent agendas of social purpose stem from commitments to

belief systems that have some degree of internal consistency — at least in the minds of adherents and advocates. Such belief systems are, in effect, the ideologies behind the major policy platforms of interest groups and, although often in a much less pure sense, behind the platforms of major political parties. Of course, national political parties must frequently 'compromise their principles' in order to attract a broad enough constituency to get members elected to regional and national governments. Nonetheless, an orientation toward one or another fundamental agenda of social purpose is usually discernible, however tarnished and compromised a party's commitment to it may be when judged on the basis of its legislative record. In the absence of any minimal commitment to a social ideology, a political party becomes 'the party of the center' or, less charitably, the party of opportunism.

Governments collect and spend taxes. Whatever specific arrangements may exist for providing particular services and regulating particular activities, every government faces the quintessentially political problem of allocating and distributing scarce and contested public resources. One can justify extracting and reallocating resources that would otherwise be consumed in the private sector only on the basis of overarching social purpose,[1] the 'public good' used generically as the justification for public sector activity. Thus every government is confronted with justifying public expenditures on the basis of one or more elements in the agenda of social purpose to which its leaders formally subscribe. In other words, no government can avoid both providing and defending a rationale for its expenditures.

In addition to the ambiguities, complications and compromises that occur as law-makers at any particular level seek to meld varying agendas of social purpose into coherent law and policy, another set of compromises is enforced by the intricate financial and policy webs which enmesh different levels of government with one another and which correspondingly decrease their freedom to act unilaterally. In such a world — the world of democratic political process — the wonder is not that governments are frequently perceived as vacillating and ineffective, but that any concerted effort of government ever occurs at all.

While pure ideological commitments are largely the prerogative — or folly — of newly formed interest groups or of fanatic, and most often marginal, fringe groups, general value sets do tend to shape the agenda of social purpose which an interest group, party or government champions. What, then, are the major competing agendas of social purpose vying for the allegiance of voters in democratic nations today? To what extent and in what ways have these agendas been affected by the technology explosion and demographic changes of the last decade? Finally, to what extent and in what ways are these agendas reflected in schooling and in the provisions people and governments make for it? Such questions are crucial for our futures as peoples and nations. Unfortunately, they are far too often answered in myopic and sterile conceptual frameworks that isolate education from wider social-policy issues.

Laissez-Faire Capitalism

Both the appeal of and the challenge to free-market capitalism have rarely been greater than at present. On the one hand, the arguments of economic efficiency advanced by supply-side economists from Adam Smith to Milton Friedman[2] seem to have acquired a new popularity and urgency in the post energy-crisis technological revolution. Business, emerging leaner and meaner from the rigors of the energy crunch and the recession which followed, has found that surviving in the world of the eighties and nineties is only possible if one keeps at the cutting edge of available technologies. And keeping on that edge inevitably means substituting technology for labour wherever possible — and increasingly that is almost everywhere.

On the other hand, the perception of a growing gap between rich and poor, has galvanized the efforts of economic interventionists to demand social policy aimed at ameliorating the circumstances of both the traditional poor and the new poor created by the micro-chip. Renewed concern for social justice in the face of massive substitution of technology for human labour leads opponents of the unfettered free-market ethos to stake out their agenda of social purpose around state intervention and control.

Social-purpose agendas are founded on beliefs about the nature of human society and the relationships within it; in fact, political statements of social purpose are really manifestos for enacting policies based on such beliefs. What are the major social purpose agendas of the political and philosophical right in the Western world today — and perhaps to an unexpected degree an important emergent social purpose agenda in soviet bloc countries as well? What assumptions and beliefs buttress these 'conservative' social goal packages?

Although the right in any country is a mixture of doctrinaire Conservatives, partisans of a moderately controlled market and society, and mid-spectrum hangers-on to the Conservative creed, a statement of their social purpose agenda would inevitably include many of the following:

- maximum market freedom consistent with minimum acceptable protection for consumers, environment and the general public
- maximum unimpeded information flow to all citizens and institutions[3]
- minimum government regulation
- minimum government intervention in markets for *all* goods and services
- moral encouragement for enterprise, entrepreneurship and self-reliance
- minimum government economic stimulation
- maximum feasible downsizing of government bureaucracies
- maximum individual choice consistent with the freedom of others to choose
- maximum self-provision for all human needs
- incentives and rewards for initiative and productivity (the meritocratic ideal)
- smaller is better, non-government is best in social-welfare programs

While this sounds like a stereotype, if not a caricature, of the archetypal conservative, it is not a bad resumé of the overall agenda of social purpose of the right. The goal is maximum personal empowerment for the greatest number. The means toward that goal is minimum interference in economic activity, in its crudest form, a social and economic Darwinism believed to provide the greatest good for the greatest number in a market as free as possible. The primary evil to be avoided in such a view is a world grown hostile to ability and effort, a nightmare world so poignantly suggested by Ayn Rand some three decades ago:

The one accusation we feared was to suspected of ability. Ability was like a mortgage on you that you could never pay off. And what was there to work for? You knew that your basic pittance would be given to you anyway, whether you worked or not — your 'housing and feeding allowance,' it was called — and above that pittance, you had no chance to get anything, no matter how hard you tried.[4]

Of course, Darwin noted that not all members of all species flourished. If the operations of the current mixed market generate inequities and injustice, however, the preferred conservative solution is not less but more personal and entrepreneurial empowerment. Indeed, in various countries and areas of social policy, Conservatives are advocating some very ingenious 'social adjustment' measures to correct for abuses they see as largely the result of past unwarranted intrusions of government into areas that ought to have been matters of private choice and concern. Some conservative American governors, for instance, recently proposed to stem the social decline in government-subsidized housing developments by providing opportunities for residents to purchase their units at highly subsidized prices, a move reminiscent of the Tory Government's sell-off of council housing to tenants in the UK. With ownership will come both responsibility and stability, champions of such policies argue. Exasperated by a long history of failure with centrally planned foreign aid programs, private entrepreneurs concerned about the misery of the world's working poor are devising ingenious schemes to provide them access to small business loans at competitive interest rates. The Tory Government in the United Kingdom looks toward government subsidy of places in the better British private schools as the last best hope for social and economic advancement of working-class children. In short, based on its own assumptions about human society, the conservative conscience, like the socialist conscience, devises its own particular remedies to the social-justice problem.

One pervasive conservative social goal is conspicuously missing from my list. It is so because, while it is consistent with the ethos of personal — and corporate — freedom, it runs directly contrary to the free-market mechanism which underpins the conservative social policy mission statement. The principle that a free world with a free market must be vigorously defended against central planning and control run amuck in eastern bloc nations has led conservatives to advocate strong defense policies — and large defense budgets to support them. Philosophical and economic conservatism has become, ironically, the soil from which the most massive market interventions in the Western world have sprung. Surely nothing distorts the goods and services markets so profoundly as the military and defense budgets of the major and minor powers of our planet. As the excesses of the arms race siphoned off more and more of the human and capital resources of the superpowers, leaders in both the United States and the Soviet Union have come to regard as insupportable the costs of such squandering of resources aimed at geometric increases in overkill capacity.

In particular, the United States has seen its competitive edge in the world marketplace severely blunted as countries without huge defense budgets overtook it in many of the most marketable areas of leading-edge technology. It is no accident that the Reagan administration began to negotiate arms control seriously when the American business community became alarmed at what the arms race was doing to their ability to compete in the world market. The fundamental anomaly of free-market doctrinaires sponsoring massive market interference to produce a completely intangible and less-and-less appreciated good (increased overkill capacity) had finally come home to roost. It had done so, ironically, because of a reasonably free world market in which many of the most economically successful nations did not interfere in their factor markets to produce huge quantities of military hardware and services. In light of widespread public recognition of such realities, simply blaming the schools for declining ability to compete in a global high-tech marketplace no longer satisfied or convinced American business.

The assumptions underpinning the conservative social purpose agenda are obvious from the very nature of that agenda.[5] The greatest good for the greatest number occurs in markets that are free of all but the most minimal safeguards for consumers, environment and the general public. Governments govern best when they govern least. In particular, bureaucracies are inherently dysfunctional and inevitably succumb to 'bureaucratic diseases', notably:

1 'Bureaucratic imperialism', their empire-building tendency.
2 Unholy alliances with factor supplies in their area of responsibility.
3 An eternal quest for absolute control, for the mandate to offer a *total* output in exchange for a total budget, that is for officially mandated monopoly.[6]
4 Waste and inefficiency.

Governments best serve their peoples by facilitating rather than directing entrepreneurial energies. Human freedom and empowerment are the paramount objectives of social policy — the *raison d'être* of free peoples and their governments everywhere. Finally, and perhaps most distinctively, conservatives believe these goals are best achieved with the least possible government intrusion into all aspects of economic and personal life.

Such beliefs, at least, would be the obvious *credo* of the perfect conservative ideologue. In democracies, of course, few ideologues of any stripe obtain the power to carry out a policy agenda based solely on *their* belief system. Most real world public-policy environments in countries with democratic institutions are a forced and uneasy marriage between the policy agendas of the right and the left. Defense is the most striking compromise (large-scale, centralized commandeering and direction of resources in the name of free-market ideology)[7] but by no means the only one. The social policy packages of democratic governments are — and ought to be — compromises subject to ongoing public scrutiny and political testing.

The second of the three discernible global social purpose 'packages' at work in the Western world today is equalitarianism, the commitment to equalizing opportunities, if not circumstances and results, in human life and affairs. This set of ideas about the proper purpose of human society, and about the policy agenda which this purpose shapes, is, in most particulars, the antithesis of *laissez-faire* capitalism. Again, the social goals of partisans of this belief system reveal their assumptions about the nature of the human situation. Again, too, pure examples of absolute commitment to such ideology are rare, in reality to be found only in the stalest of structural Marxist circles.

Equalitarianism, The Quest for Equity

While the right seeks primarily to maximize freedom and choice, the left seeks mainly to equalize indicators of human well-being. The indicators selected are many and diverse, although fortunately reducible to three basic categorical types. The principle of equality of opportunity suggests that circumstances external to individuals should not limit their choices and options in significant matters affecting their well-being (access to heart surgery, for instance, should not be a function of income). Unfortunately, no way exists to measure an opportunity. Therefore, equalitarians have turned to attempting to measure treatments or results as the best available surrogates for opportunity.

Measuring and comparing treatments in important areas of social policy, however, is rarely any more practical than trying to put numbers to opportunities. How, for instance, can we determine with certainty the qualitative differences among different types of public housing in different types of neighbourhoods with different types of residents? Is an $80,000 townhouse with a large garden space better than, say, a $50,000 apartment in a neighbourhood with better golf courses — and for whom? In the absence of a market process to quantify perceived values (what economists call 'utilities') as a price which results or would likely result in a sale, we are always left to judge apples and oranges.[8]

One 'treatment' in social policy is, however, quantifiable — money. It is also the focus of intense interest on the part of nearly everyone up and down the social policy ladder. For this reason money has become the principal working gauge used by interventionists of all stripes to meter and monitor equalization, the one workable surrogate for their favourite idea of what needs to be equalized among members of society and groups in society. In moments of serious reflection, of course, even politicans or policy advocates deeply committed to equalitarian principles recognize that equalizing money does not necessarily equalize anything else — but what else can they put numbers to that everyone takes seriously?

Trying to equalize results (or outcomes) is certainly no help. Headstart programs aimed at helping poor children develop social and academic skills to improve their future educational and life-chances, for example, require twenty or thirty-year longitudinal research projects to assess. More to the point, they require agreement on what 'better' life outcomes are. Once again the evaluator is left to sort, compare and judge infinitely diverse, complex and varied life outcomes. Such comparisons and judgments must ultimately be grounded in the evaluator's beliefs and values bearing on the nature of the common and individual good.

Despite ongoing efforts by those who, against all odds, valiantly pursue the Holy Grail of 'objectively comparable standards' for evaluating social policy, politicians who must cut their tax pie in some way they can defend in terms of equity, rarely have faith in any measures except budgets and headcounts (unless, perhaps, a particular study supports *their* favourite social policy agenda). As a result, the pursuit of equity usually resolves itself into complex intersector (public/private) and intergovernmental equalization and transfer schemes which translate a formal rationale of purpose into fiscal formulae. These are typically inscrutable to all but the initiated and thus advocates of competing social purpose agendas tend to use them interchangeably to advance their own particular reform programs.

Two basic problems confront the would-be equalizer, once he or she has finally gotten round to budgets and money. First, people and organizations with the same sum of money available for a particular commodity or service can buy different amounts or different qualities of it. Second, people or organizations buying the same amount and quality of something may need or want different amounts or qualities of it (e.g., not everyone 'needs' a seven-bedroom house or sufficient mathematical education to solve differential equations deftly). Of course, deciding who needs what is inescapably subjective and value-laden, but arbitrating battles over need perceptions is, nonetheless, the essence of a major portion of political life.

The more we try to equalize dollar inputs and give the same relative 'spending power' to government jurisdictions, organizations and individuals, the less we take into account differences in costs and need. *To equalize perfectly is to ignore differences.* Everyone gets a red Ford Tempo. To set compensatory spending levels only on the basis of need perceptions, however, gives Porsches to those who prepare the best briefs on why they need Porsches — and used bicycles to those who can't argue their particular need perceptions convincingly in the political forum. *Virtually all real-world equalization efforts are a compromise between equalizing spending power on the one hand, and differentiating it on the basis of perceived needs on the other.*[9]

Life, then, is not simple for equalitarians. Behind their attractive slogans of fairness for all lies a quagmire of definitional complexity and policy ambiguity. Except in terms of brute data on budget dollars spent, the definitional ground they stand on is perpetually shifting and threatening to give way under them. Budget numbers, after all, do not speak for themselves any more than research data.[10] They too must be interpreted — and budget numbers that provide excellent support for a claim that equalization targets have been met can always be turned on end with a different set of assumptions about what is right and good — or even just tolerable. Despite the difficulties associated with attempts to equalize the outputs of social policy programs, however, the political pressure to do so is a permanent feature of all public policy fields and at all levels of governance. From the advent of compulsory, universal schooling in the late nineteenth century, until recently, it has been generally taken for granted, for instance, that equality of opportunity involved maintaining publicly operated and universally available school systems, systems whose mission was extended during the 1960s to include providing all essential knowledge for every type of student — in the same manner that equal opportunity to mail delivery was taken to imply a state postal system. At the extremes, of course, consensus may exist that some equalization is necessary and desirable. Even among the most ardent Conservative ideologues, few would agree with Scrooge that starving in the cold should be allowed to perform its Malthusian function of 'decreasing the surplus population' while 10 per cent of the population lives in opulence undreamed of by emperors of yore. Yet some, not a few in fact, would deny that state-administered social programs designed to better the life circumstances of even the most oppressed and impoverished are a desirable and feasible way of doing so. Better, committed small-c conservatives argue, to turn over the *delivery and administration* of such compensatory services to small local independent agencies close to beneficiaries. Better still if the programs themselves are shaped and tailored locally. Best of all if the resources required come from close-to-the-problem grass-roots concern.

Nonetheless, the perception of gross problems in equity, in fundamental social justice, is widespread in human society generally — as is the belief that individuals and private corporations — will not do enough of the right kind of things for those who suffer in our midst. This belief leads to the argument that only government with its taxing power can assure a minimal flow of the right kinds of goods and services to those who would otherwise perish as part of social and economic evolution. The classic economic argument for public provision of services, after all, is that some or many individuals will lack the means, information or desire to purchase a minimal acceptable amount and quality of a particular good or service — *and that public well-being and economic productivity will suffer as a result.* People who starve in the cold, after all, do not always do so quietly. In large numbers, they threaten not only productivity but the economic and social order as a whole. In lesser numbers they may spread disease, drugs and depredation. In short, they are bad for the rule of law — and bad for business.

To minimize this type of damage to the 'public good', governments become involved in minimally redistributive efforts to equalize such private goods as housing and food and such mixed goods (benefiting both individuals and the public) as health care and education. Governments keep such efforts minimally redistributive because they must ultimately avoid fostering a flight of capital and business by taxing too heavily. Nonetheless, some sort of social safety net is usually conceded as desirable by all but the most doctrinaire conservative thinkers. And implementing a social safety net involves, even if the service delivery were entrusted entirely to the private sector, trying to equalize spending power for selected goods and services. For this reason, even the most conservative regimes typically budget funds to allow their poor to obtain vital services and goods they would otherwise lack. The amount and quality of the equalization may be little more than an empty gesture, but the gesture is rarely omitted.

The equalitarian zealot, a pure believer in the ability of government to orchestrate the well-being of its citizens, would endorse a social purpose agenda along the following lines:

- maximum equalization of opportunity, treatment and outcomes consistent with whatever minimum protection of choice will be demanded by those who have the economic and political power to limit equalization
- maximum government regulation
- extensive government protection for consumers and environment
- maximum government intervention ('planning', 'rationalization') in markets for *all* goods and services
- maximum standardization of public services
- maximum government economic stimulation
- toleration of, and support for, government bureaucracies proportional to their expanded control mandate
- maximum government power to prescribe similar opportunities, treatment and outcomes for all
- minimum self-provision for all human needs
- bigger is better; government knows best in social welfare programs since it can achieve the greatest 'economies of scale' and standardization

Not surprisingly, this agenda is nearly the mirror image of the idealized conservative social policy agenda presented on p. 8. In pure form, such a social purpose agenda reveals a central focus on making the conditions people experience in life, if not the people themselves, as much alike as possible. The goal is maximum sameness at least of opportunity, ideally of treatment and outcomes as well. The principal evil to be avoided is unconscionable disparity in wealth, income and living standard which equalitarians attribute to free-market capitalism. They see big government as the key to such equalized opportunity and life chances.

When equalitarians are confronted with bureaucratic inefficiency and a lack of evidence that existing equalization programs have greatly homogenized human circumstances, they typically respond that real equalization has never been tried and therefore its merits are unknown. More fundamentally, they easily commit what Sanders has recently and aptly labelled the 'moralistic fallacy', accepting what one wishes were true — what one considers would be true in a 'better' world — as if it were.[11] The equalitarian desire for equality of opportunity, treatment and results easily becomes a wish that all people were the same, or even a belief that they are. After all, large centralized social programs would be much more workable if we all shared the same values, beliefs and characteristics — or would such programs ultimately be unnecessary in a world of clones?

More sameness, in the equalitarian agenda, is simply better than more diversity. Here the ultimate and dominant goal is equality, not choice and diversity. Moreover, by invoking the moralistic fallacy, the committed equalitarian comes to the conclusion that, because people ought to be the same, they are.[12] Furthermore — and better yet from the equalitarian perspective — because people are the same, they should respond to equal treatment with equal results. Therefore, giving people the same education and health care, for instance, should make them equally knowledgable and healthy. What is missing, of course, in this caricature of left-leaning thought is the reality of human differences. For better and for worse, whether the result of nature or nurture, such differences exist and cannot be willed away. We may all be equal in some limited legal or philosophical sense, but we are manifestly not the same, each of us being marked and shaped by our genetic make-up, social environment and cultural heritage. In many cases that shaping process is, by any humane standard, tragic, but it is real and it produces profound and deeply rooted differences in the way people understand and cope with their existence.

The two major opposite social purpose agendas of *laissez-faire* conservativism and equalitarianism embrace and integrate areas of belief about social purpose that anyone must confront who thinks seriously about why we are as a society and what we ought to try to become. Ultimately, anyone seeking to pass judgment on social policy issues, must, explicitly or implicitly, deal with the relative desirability of standardized treatment versus unfettered human and corporate initiative. Various supporters of these two diametrically opposed social policy camps have different degrees of commitment to different agenda items, but what makes them distinguishable politically from their opponents is an overall orientation in one direction or the other. Of course, parties of the middle continue to pick and choose from both menus and to suggest specific real-world compromises between the two absolutist policy agendas.[13]

Structural Pluralism

A third major unifying social purpose agenda has emerged, however, in the last two decades. While supporters of this agenda can and do pick and choose among items in the social policy creeds of the other two camps, they represent, I believe, a distinctively different orientation toward social purpose. The context in which this pattern of political commitment has emerged fits better in the following chapter on social policy contexts. The prescriptions for social policy and the gestalt of belief behind them, however, belong here.

An important thread of political thought and commitment today — one that is clearly much more recent than the other two major threads of *laissez-faire* capitalism and equalitarianism — is an orientation toward the preservation of fundamental cultural, and even language-use, differences in a pluralistic society. Frequently this view of what we ought to become as peoples and nations is accompanied by a commitment to structural pluralism: different institutions for different groups in society. What sense can there be, advocates of structural pluralism argue, in imposing on minorities institutions which both confuse and alienate them?

As with the two other major popularly understood agendas of social purpose, a *pure* commitment to pluralist principles at the expense of all other social policy goals is a mindset of the fanatic and rarely to be seen in regional and national political arenas. Nonetheless, for clarification and argument, here is a menu of 'pure' pluralist social policy goal priorities:

- cultural and language differences are to be preserved
- minority languages and cultures are to have the opportunity to adapt and develop
- separate cultures deserve separate institutions
- legal definition of and protection for group as well as for individual rights
- group welfare is at least equal to if not superior to that of individuals
- where they conflict, group rights should prevail

Laissez-faire capitalism and equalitarianism frequently coexist with an assumption that public policy should foster overall cultural and linguistic unity. Partisans of either conservative or equalitarian principles are quite capable of insisting that minimum acceptable social cohesiveness requires at least a single (or very small number) of languages of use, and at best the relatively unified cultural milieu of the melting-pot ideal. Conservatives, for their part, can argue that national markets work most efficiently with consensus about fundamental value issues, and in one language. Equalitarians already troubled by the difficulty of equating apples and oranges, have no desire, at least not on the basis of their own agenda of principle, to encourage further and more profound differences which can only make equity judgments more like comparing apples and micro-chips.

There is much, moreover, in the other two social purpose creeds which pluralists can and do appropriate for their own purposes — which is to say that pluralists will take positions to the right or left as they see fit. On the one hand, the promise of the free-market ideal of choice and diversity seems to offer just what pluralists want, the freedom to be different. On the other, an abundance of sociological evidence demonstrates that certain minorities fare very poorly indeed in relatively free market conditions. Hence pluralism, particularly for oppressed minorities, evokes demands for such equalitarian, interventionist policies as compensatory and affirmative-action programs.

The main problem with pushing social and cultural pluralism too far, opponents argue, is that societies can lose the critical mass of social cohesion which makes possible both peaceful co-existence and economic survival and competitiveness. Pluralists meet this challenge with their observation that forced assimilation has a very poor international track record for establishing peace, harmony and productivity. Instead, they appeal to the ideal of a cohesive diversity.[14] National societies are strongest and best integrated, they insist, when cultures and languages coexist in mutual respect — and most vulnerable when a dominant group creates social policy aimed at assimilating minorities against their will.

The Agenda of Schooling

Such are the three principal belief systems behind the three major *popularly recognized and understood* social purpose and policy agendas at work in the world today. It would be surprising if these had no counterparts in agendas for the control and delivery of schooling. In fact, they do. Each set of priorities has a counterpart in the educational policy arena, and at all levels. What we believe society ought to do for its members and what we believe it ought to become, after all, has everything to do with what we believe about schooling. The schooling agendas which flow from fundamental mind sets about social purpose is the main business of this book. These agendas in the minds of social and educational policy-makers lead them to alternative ideas about how schooling should be conceived, financed and delivered.

Those whose ideological roots are in the free-market tradition look for ways and means to make schooling less a matter of state policy and more a matter of individual choice. To be sure, such an orientation can lead to manifold complications and contradictions, more choice for the few, for instance, and no choice at all for the many, but the response of policy-makers to practical policy problems is almost never to change ideology. Instead, the search of conservative policy-makers continues for ways and means to realize the benefits of more privatized educational delivery arrangements.

Those whose ideological roots are equalitarian search among the problems evident in large publicly administered and controlled education systems for clues to how they might develop a perfectly standardized and controlled public system that is fair, free and equal. They argue the dangers to those who are most disadvantaged educationally of a 'deregulated' and largely private educational arena. In a deregulated and privatized educational arena, who, they ask, will provide 'equal education' — or any education at all — for the poor, especially the inner-city poor, and for those in remote areas? Who will run schools where vast government-subsidized operating deficits are the only conceivable means of institutional survival? Who will provide for the special needs — often astronomically expensive needs — of special children? Who will set standards and evaluate against them to provide some assurance of quality and comparability in educational services?

The questions are many and consequential, but for each the conservative ideologue has an answer drawn from his or her own particular agenda of social purpose. The poor for whom education is a real priority will make the necessary sacrifices as they already do in surprising numbers,[15] the committed conservative argues, to get an education for their children and that education will be all the better for it. Those who can run such schools efficiently, and hence profitably, will provide for the needs of special learners, proponents of conservative education policies in general and privatization in particular insist, and schools surviving solely because of vast government subsidies and compulsory attendance laws ought not, in any case, to be preserved since they serve neither private nor the public good. For their part, of course, committed equalitarians see such conservative responses to their concerns about social and educational equity as at best naive and at worst dishonest.

Finally, those committed to a pluralistic vision of society look for schooling arrangements which foster diversity within an atmosphere of mutual respect. They veer in the direction of deregulation and privatization when they view such policies as enhancing the chances of 'cohesive diversity' rather than undesired assimilation. When large-system standardization seems the more appropriate tool at hand, however, pluralists become advocates of equalitarian social and educational policies. Pluralist social and educational policy frequently produces strange political bedfellows indeed.

Conclusion

Three things seem evident from the preceding discussion. First, educational policy and practice should not be considered outside some framework for understanding the major, global and popularly understood ideologies of social purpose which drive social policy debate. Education is a part — a fiercely contested and symbolically central part — of overall social policy, but it is only a part of the whole. Second, advocates of 'pure versions' of ideological agendas rarely succeed in gaining acceptance of those agendas in democratic political life, and so most social policy packages in democratically governed countries are a strained compromise — or, more positively, a dynamic tension — among major competing views of desirable social destinies. The same tension and ambivalence is omnipresent in the ways we provide for schooling. These are, however, dynamic tensions and the balance among basic social priorities appears to be shifting considerably in many technologically advanced nations, in large measure tilted from its former relative equilibrium by fundamental changes in the environment of learning and work.

Third, social purpose agendas, driven by value commitments to particular views of the 'good society' and how to achieve it, spawn new and ever-changing alternatives to current governance and finance arrangements for all manner of public-sector or mixed activities. The evolution of proposals for alternative arrangements for health, education and welfare are limited only by the imagination, and sense of political acceptability, of those with voice in public affairs. In recent years, the imagination of social critics and policy-makers has been particularly fecund in devising, and often testing, alternative arrangements for schooling.

These three conclusions provide an agenda of purpose for the remainder of this book. First, major changes have occurred in the way work is done, in the realities of the world economy, in the context of schooling and in the way we regard society at large. Chapter 3 sketches these changes and their impact on the way we think about schooling. Chapter 4 examines two frameworks for understanding schooling arrangements and Chapters 5 and 6 outline the major generic types of alternative learning arrangements being suggested and tested internationally. Chapter 7 presents and critiques the principal claims and counterclaims of advocates and opponents of more privatization in education. Chapter 8 examines issues and claims surrounding the education of special populations in the evolving context of social purpose perceptions. Finally, the concluding chapter considers educational futures in light of the major, widely-understood agendas of social purpose, of available alternatives, and of the issues these alternative approaches raise.

Notes

1   Taxes inevitably impose a 'dead weight loss' on economic activity and are everywhere recognized an inhibiting economic activity which might occur in their absences. For a straightforward discussion of this 'excess burden', see Richard A. Musgrave and Peggy B. Musgrave *Public Finance in Theory and Practice* (New York: McGraw-Hill Book Co., 1980), pp. 304–5 and pp. 318–19.

2   For a clear summary of the ethos behind contemporary free-market capitalism, see Milton Friedman, *Capitalism and Freedom* (Chicago: University of Chicago Press, 1962), especially pp. 12–21. Many of the same basic arguments for the economic efficiency of a free-market system were advanced by Adam Smith two centuries ago. See Adam Smith, *An Inquiry into the Nature and Causes of The Wealth of Nations*, ed. Bruce Mazlish (1776; reprint, New York: Bobbs-Merrill, 1961), especially pp. 55–62. For a particularly scathing attack on the ill-effects of interventionism on free-market capitalism see Rodney Atkinson, *Government Against the People: The Economics of Political Exploitation* (Southampton: The Camelot Press, 1986), pp. 46–57.

3   Of course, those who desire and can afford 'better' information should, in this agenda, be free to produce it — and retain it as a proprietary right. The only exception would be information indisputably necessary to public safety or well-being.

4   Ayn Rand, *Atlas Shrugged* (New York: Random House, 1957), p. 663.

5   See summary of social purpose agenda of the political right, page 8.

6   Adapted from E. West 'The public monopoly and the seeds of self-destruction', in *Family Choice in Schooling* ed. Michael Manley-Casimir (Toronto: D.C. Heath and Company, 1981), pp. 185–98.

7   Howevermuch competition and free-market dynamics may be exploited in pursuit of a large-scale military defense initiative such as the American Strategic Defense Initiative, mounting such a project is inescapably a mammoth exercise in centralized government planning.

8   Despite perennial administrative rhetoric to conceal the fact, that is equally true in education. As soon as one party argues that equal treatment consists in doing one thing (say streaming our schools into ability groups), another will rise to contend that really equal treatment demands something very different — even the very opposite (such as a 'common curriculum' for all).

9   In the jargon of public finance, *horizontal equity* seeks to treat those perceived to be equal as equals (thus offering the same 'spending power' for all), while *vertical equity* seeks to treat those perceived to be unequal unequally (more money for those with greater needs or higher costs).

10 See p. 5.

11 Sanders points out that the naturalistic fallacy, taking what is and assuming that it ought to be is often reversed, a pattern of thought he has labelled the 'moralistic fallacy'. He does so in James Sanders, 'From ought to is: Radwanski and the moralistic fallacy', in *Reform and Relevance in Schooling: Dropouts, Destreaming and the Common Curriculum*, eds Derek Allison and Jerry Paquette (Toronto: OISE Press, in press).

12 The ideological offspring of this perspective in education is the 'mastery learning' principle — virtually all students can learn anything if given time and properly paced and sequenced learning activities — an influential theory proposed by Jerome Bruner almost three decades ago. See Jerome Bruner, *The Process of Education* (Boston: Harvard University Press, 1960; Toronto: Vintage Books, 1963), pp. 33–54. More recently the same belief has given rise to the 'common curriculum' movement. For one particularly celebrated statement of this belief and a complete educational policy agenda derived from it, see Mortimer J. Adler, *The Paideia Proposal: An Educational Manifesto* (New York: Macmillan, 1982), pp. 41–5.

13 These poles are in fact spanned by a spectrum of political commitments ranging from anti-collectivism through what Dennis Lawton calls 'reluctant collectivism' to Fabian socialists and Marxists and other 'comprehensive planners'. Denis Lawton, 'Ideologies of education', in *The National Curriculum*, eds Denis Lawton and Clyde Chitty (London: Billing and Sons, 1988), pp. 10–20.

14 This term has appeared recently in various places. My earliest encounter with it was in reports of various United Church of Canada policy discussions. The claim, however, that toleration and even encouragement of diversity may enhance rather than endanger social cohesion is a pervasive one among those committed to social and structural pluralism.

15 In the United States, for instance, evidence exists that, with increasing statistical frequency, inner-city working poor are spending up to 10 per

cent of their annual family income to give their children a chance they believe they can never have in inner-city public schools. Virgil Blum, in 'Why inner-city families send their children to private schools: An empirical study', in *Private Schools and the Public Good: Policy Alternatives for the Eighties*, ed. Edward M. Gaffney (Notre Dame: University of Notre Dame Press, 1981), pp. 17–24, provides some surprising statistics in this regard.

Chapter 3

Changing the Rules of the Social Policy Game

Old rules serve players very poorly in a new game — especially when the stakes are as high as cultural, economic and political survival. One does not have to be a futurist to recognize that some long-standing and fundamental rules of the social policy game have dramatically changed in the post-war decades — and not just for some nations, not just, for instance, for technologically advanced capitalist countries — but for all. The changes have been different for less-developed nations and peoples, but none the less important because they have taken a somewhat different form there. Not even the iron curtain has proven a sufficient shield against major changes in the context of work and in the cultural fabric of the peoples who make up the nations of this planet.

Even while the way we work — and to a very considerable extent *who* works and at what — has been radically altered, the cultural and racial homogeneity of nation states has dissolved before the combined influences of modern communication, transportation and a world economy which provides both the incentives and means for mass migrations in many different directions at once. Traditional arrangements for rearing and educating children are everywhere under great stress as governments seek to understand and react to massive and almost instantaneous changes in who and what their peoples are and how they work.

In the midst of such change, those concerned with social policy issues are confronted with a flood of research evidence emanating from the 1960s and early 1970s which documented massive social stratification by class in Western democracies, a stratification which evidently reproduces itself generation after generation and a stratification, moreover, in which schools of all sorts appear to play a key role.[1] In short, just as new and largely unforeseen changes started to rewrite radically the rules of social policy, we began to comprehend that policies touted as 'social equalizers' had reinforced — or at least failed to eliminate — classes of winners and losers in society. Furthermore, available evidence suggested that, even with universal, compulsory education, very little movement occurred among those classes from one generation to the next. Even before futurists started pointing unrelentingly to the fateful impact of micro-electronics on whatever cultural and economic destiny we might face, critical theorists were forcing policy-makers to think about previously unknown concepts such as social reproduction, resistance and cultural capital.

What has changed in the context of work and schooling — and in the way we perceive them? How do these changes interact with the major agendas of social purpose which are all the more vehemently debated as these changes force themselves on the awareness of governments and their citizenry?

Demography: Who We Are

As never before large numbers of people are on the move across the world. Although accurate and comparable numbers are virtually impossible to obtain, it seems certain that, in absolute numbers, recent migrations dwarf the colonial migrations of the last three centuries. The trend to massive population shifts has occurred for a number of reasons and these reasons have changed considerably over the last three decades. War and persecution have always ranked high among the reasons people forsake their homeland, and the current international crisis in identifying and accommodating refugees suggests that their importance has diminished little in the last twenty years.

But displacement by war and oppression have been overtaken by other motivations for emigration. During the boom years of the 1960s, industrialized nations competing in labour-intensive manufacturing sectors developed an all but insatiable appetite for unskilled and moderately-skilled labour to work their assembly lines. During this period mass immigration — often conceived as 'temporary' — was the preferred solution to this labour demand, particularly in Europe. Thus began the 'migrant worker' phenomenon as a fact of social and political life in the major European industrial nations.

While the high-tech revolution in manufacturing is largely a phenomenon of the 1970s and 1980s, production during the boom years was dependent on an adequate supply of engineers and technicians. Countries slow to expand technical education at the university and vocational-institute level were forced to look elsewhere for a pool of technically competent persons to design and run their manufacturing establishments. Thus, in countries like Canada, immigration policies began to favour those with specific technical skills useful in the manufacturing sector. Furthermore, in some countries, and again Canada is a good example, the very fact of relatively open immigration policies during the boom years expanded demand in the service sector, including the public-service sector, faster than domestic education and training programs could meet it. The 'recruiting trip' to England for qualified school teachers, for instance, was a regular feature of administrative life in many Canadian school boards during those halcyon years.

The most enduring legacy of such policies for the industrialized nations of the world was a fundamentally changed racial and cultural fabric. For the most part 'migrant' workers had either no desire to return to their homelands, or simply nothing to return to there. Long after the economic rationale for the presence of many less-skilled migrants in host countries had ceased to exist, the migrants remained, and continue to remain. Compounding the problem of migrant workers whose former economic usefulness had disappeared, was the arrival in ever-growing numbers of refugees and illegal immigrants, an influx made easy, as well as difficult to stop, by ubiquitous and relatively inexpensive air travel and occasionally, as in the case of the south-western United States, by a border shared between a rich and poor nation.

No social melting pot proved hot enough, however, to assimilate these waves of the poor, the oppressed, the unskilled and the culturally different. Many minorities remained not only unassimilated but manifestly resistant to the very idea of assimilation. Only in the face of an evident failure of assimilationist social and educational policies did governments gradually begin abandoning them.[2] While some minorities blended into majority social and cultural milieus relatively successfully — indeed, a few with remarkable success — many, especially those whose cultural differences were greatest, simply did not 'fit in' and lived a ghettoized sub-culture.

Among the poor nations, increased access to emigration provided the mixed blessing of a social safety valve that also, however, entailed a loss of many relatively educated and ambitious persons who might otherwise have remained in their native land. Thus, many poor nations have found themselves in the unenviable position of providing very scarce higher educational resources to many who ultimately go elsewhere to live and work. Moreover, they are forced to do so at a time when they are trying to repay crushing national debts in a world market which allocates mainly menial, low-paying jobs to their populace and *therefore provides a much better rate of public return on primary school education than on higher education.*[3]

Of no small interest in these global rearrangements of populations is the relative immunity Pacific-rim countries have enjoyed from mass immigration. While certain among them (Japan and China) have contributed markedly to immigration to diverse Western nations in the post-war period, they were themselves, for several reasons, insulated from large-scale immigration and its social policy implications. Doubtlessly, it would be unreasonable to attribute the recent industrial, high-tech and educational success of certain Pacific rim countries, especially Japan, solely to the relative stability of their demographic make-up, yet it is certainly an important social variable which sets these 'recently industrialized' countries apart from Western industrial powers.

A new, relatively small but potentially very significant, wave of immigration has recently descended upon Western industrialized nations increasingly concerned by the growing economic hegemony of Japan and, to a lesser extent, of Hong Kong and Korea. We have arrived at an era of immigration policies tailored to encourage immigration of wealthy entrepreneurs from other lands — increasingly from the east, a process recently accelerated by the imminent transfer of Hong Kong to China. In countries like Canada and Australia explicit immigration policies encourage such importation of capital *cum* entrepreneurialism. This new wave of immigration establishes 'ethnic communities' which are virtually the exact opposite in all respects of the more traditional enclaves of struggling immigrants in largely hostile lands. Instead of third-class communities of families struggling to find subsistence in a strange and largely inscrutable cultural and economic milieu, we have emerging communities of powerful owner-entrepreneurs who have proven their mettle in the savagely free markets of the east. Far from being 'educationally disadvantaged', such persons often combine high levels of formal education with the insider's penchant for understanding national and international markets grown increasingly 'ethnic'. Not to be forgotten among those who have come from the east to the Western industrial powers are those who have been sent to take over and manage floundering industrial (not to mention real property) dinosaurs according to the culture, beliefs and practices of Japanese business. In brief, a new wave of short-term and long-term immigration has served to raise the fear that the Western industrial community is in imminent danger of economic eclipse, if not of literal take-over, in the high-tech information economy of the coming decades.

In the midst of massive immigration-driven changes in the demographic composition of Western industrial nations has come a generalized and precipitous decline in birthrates. Not only has the technology of contraception been reduced to pill taking (albeit by only one of the two human genders) or a short out-patient procedure, the quest for a better standard of living has led more couples everywhere (except again in Japan, where women are only beginning to enter the permanent labour force) to seek employment for both marriage partners, to delay having children and to have fewer of them than ever before. While certain countries and regions have reached birthrates that are remarkably low even in a field of birthrates far below the replacement level, all the major western industrial powers have experienced dramatic reductions in fertility rates over the last generation.

The result of relatively open immigration policies and below-replacement-level birthrates is that the original or founding peoples of most Western technologically advanced nations now fear becoming strangers in their own lands. Recent unavowedly or even overtly racist movements in the political arenas of certain European countries can be linked directly to this sense of an imminent danger of reverse assimilation from within one's 'own' country, an outcome paradoxically reminiscent of the fate of Aboriginal peoples overrun by European colonists. In one jurisdiction — interestingly one that has achieved the very lowest birthrate in the world in recent years — a government is currently seeking by public policy to reverse this trend. In response to demographic data indicating that those with French as a home language had declined to less than half of the Quebec population, the government of that province has resorted to generous baby bonuses in the hope of improving the fecundity of its populace.[4]

Beyond and within the altered ethnic and cultural face of our countries and peoples is the problem of widespread family breakdown. The nuclear family is not only under heavy fire, it has, in some regions, become a minority arrangement for living and for rearing children. Increasingly half or more of the children in national societies are being raised by one parent, most often a mother who must, at best, make do with one rather than two incomes and who frequently must live and raise her children in abject poverty. The traditional helping role of the extended family, moreover, in rearing and in-culcating a strong value set in children, has disappeared as extended family ties have been severed in extremely urban and mobile societies.

For better or for worse, we are not what we once were: and all indications are that we can never return from whence we came. The reality of profound and widespread demographic change, in particular the emergence of national and even regional societies that are amal-gams of diverse peoples, is one that can only have the deepest effects on our sense of social purpose and on the policies we spin from that basic goal agenda. In a very real way, the recent ascendency of pluralism as an espoused political agenda is a reaction to this percep-tion that we are no longer single peoples in single nations, but that all of us have become culturally what only the unnatural and volatile national amalgams of central Europe were in former times: many peoples in one state. Equally, such fundamental change in who we are must have the most far-reaching implications for our sense of educa-tional purpose. Education is, after all, a primordial social symbol viewed by many as a sort of social sacrament, something which accomplishes what it symbolizes. Schools are central, highly visible symbols of social purpose and hence, 'whatever else they are, and whether we like it or not, schools are arenas in which the deepest conflicts within the societies they are meant both to reproduce and change are played out'.[5]

Nor are important changes in the demographic make-up of industrialized nations limited to culture and language. Dramatically reduced birthrates on the heels of post-war baby booms have left industrialized Western countries with rapidly ageing populations, populations in which youth will soon confer a minority status of its own. The significance of the ageing of national populations in terms of our sense of social purpose can hardly be overestimated. The graying-population phenomenon places political clout in the hands of the aged and creates an inverted population pyramid in which relative-ly few tax-payers and pension plan contributors will soon have to support a much larger cohort of elderly. Furthermore, this ageing baby-boom cohort seems likely to live longer than any previous generation and hence to make even greater demands on health care systems and pension funds than would otherwise have been the case. In such a public-policy scenario, some very difficult trade-offs will face politicians as they seek to apply their belief systems to the most practical and perhaps most consequential of political problems, budget-making.

Technology and Automation

Few, if any, technologies of work have survived the last two decades without radical transformation. Many, if not most, of what were once skilled trades and crafts have now been largely reduced to robotic routines. From the most menial to the most lofty, work is now almost universally assisted and even underpinned by a configuration of microchip technology that was only a Rube Goldberg dream — or nightmare — two decades ago. Today one simply cannot, it seems, afford the time or the risk of preparing a list, fixing a car or making a managerial decision without intervention and assistance from high technology. Moreover, whole new repertoires of specifically high-technology work have evolved to support an apparently insatiable appetite for hardware and software to expand and facilitate productive capacities. Of course, however diverse and impressive the repertoire of new high-tech occupations may be, the number of persons employed in them is relatively small — especially when compared with the number of persons robotics and other technologies have displaced from traditional unskilled, low and medium-skilled occupations — and recently from lower and middle-management positions as well. Even within the high-tech employment dossier itself, moreover, opportunities are far from limitless as the recent American rush to supply an apparently 'insatiable' demand for computer workers and engineers (estimated at 40,000 a year by the Task Force of the Business-Higher Education Forum in 1983) demonstrated. 'Unfortunately, by 1986 sectors of the electronics industry were laying off workers in a period of economic recovery, sorry news for students who rushed to computer majors ...'[6]

The principal socioeconomic effect of the high-tech revolution has in fact been to erode the occupational foundations of the lower, and increasingly the middle, middle class. Gone are low- and medium-skilled (but modestly well-remunerated) positions in manufacturing that require mainly rote manual skills. Unmistakably going are low-discretion lower and middle-level management positions which require mainly programmable decisions that do not require human insight and intuition. The flowering of high technology has fostered an immense credentialling fissure between low-level service occupations — the general employment residue of the high-tech revolution — and occupations which require some degree of human attention, insight and intuition. On one side of that gap are non-credentialled occupations, basic retailing, cleaning and manual labour tasks — in a word, 'Mcjobs'. On the other, rests virtually all other work, which increasingly carries a formal requirement for considerable post-secondary education. After surveying the literature on the emerging American labour market, Perrow has concluded that job-creation in low-level service industries will far outstrip that elsewhere and that the occupations with the greatest immediate growth potential are 'janitors, nurses aides and orderlies, sales clerks, cashiers, and waiters and waitresses'.[7] In short, those who fall between the categories of no credentials and highly credentialled, and this has been and generally remains the majority of persons in Western democracies, will increasingly have no employment options beyond the most basic and menial of occupational tasks — and even these are by no means secure from the 'improvements' which technology may soon bring to them (for example, in emerging robotic fast-food restaurants).

Schools, of course, are a key component in this credentialling process as numerous radical critics have been quick to point out. This demand for credentialling, moreover, seems singularly unlikely to abate in societies so deeply dependent on multitudinous technologies. No one without a strong gambling instinct or death wish, for instance, (presumably not even radical education critics) would seriously suggest abolishing certification of, say, aircraft mechanics or doctors. This is so, despite the fact that certification is a relatively unreliable surrogate for control over the quality of work. Imperfect as it is, however, it remains one of the better *available* quality-control mechanisms. In short, credentialling, and the escalation of credentials, appears to be here to stay. Moreover, *they would persist even if people and policy-makers generally accepted the radical view of credentialling as a process by which the schools, and other public and private agencies, legitimize the continual reduction of available desirable employment.* Universally accepted industrial and service-sector goals of safety (especially for the consumer), reliability and efficiency would require enhancement rather than diminution of credentialling.

The greatest immediate significance of this radical escalation of formal, academically-based credentialling to the evolution of schooling is increasing awareness among the young that any personal occupational payoff for them in schooling beyond the most minimal literacy and numeracy skills becomes available *only at the end of a difficult, high-demand post-secondary program of some sort.* A quantum jump of credentialling, and of higher education needed to obtain that credentialling, has intervened between the 'typical secondary student' and work that provides a decent standard of living. A little more education no longer equals a little better job. The smooth, approximately linear relationship between education and income assumed in older human-capital ideas of educational contribution to productivity and earning no longer applies. It needs to be reconceptualized as the quantum-like step-function it has, in fact, become. Current wide-spread concern over high drop-out rates and poor standards may indicate more than anything else that students, and the young generally, have a better sense than their elders of this quantumization of economic and job-satisfaction rewards at the end of the schooling rainbow. Since meaningful payoff in terms of interesting and reasonably well-paid work is increasingly only for those who run the full educational mile, young people drop out of school sooner rather than later unless firmly convinced that they can be, and want to be, educational long-distance runners.

The snowballing of leading-edge technologies that change most work from labour-intensive to capital-intensive presents a truly unprecedented challenge to our sense of social, and educational, purpose. The logic of the technological imperative in business and industry is, after all, ruthlessly Darwinian. Whatever moral inclination an owner or manager may have to preserve employment, failure to increase productivity by maximizing reliance on technology and minimizing reliance on human labour is a self-imposed corporate death warrant. *The end result of refusing to adopt and adapt the new technologies is not more jobs but no jobs at all.*

The impetus of this high-tech imperative leads clearly to a new kind of society and constitutes a fundamental challenge to our basic agendas of social purpose before which the upheaval of the industrial revolution may well pale. How will we design a just or fair society, or more modestly even a minimally acceptable society, if it becomes evident that meaningful work is increasingly the preserve of the very, very few? What if the current trend toward scarcity of meaningful full-time employment even for the highly credentialled becomes, as it seems it must, far more serious than it currently is? What bases will we use for the allocation, distribution and redistribution of scarce resources when individual contribution to economic productivity can sensibly be applied as a criterion only to a tiny cadre of technocrats who themselves must share their work as computers come to handle much of the work even of designing better computers? What can we equalize — and why and how in such a brave new world? The technological revolution poses fundamental questions of social purpose which do not easily fit into the traditional goal agendas of democratic peoples.

Some futurists point optimistically to the potential for liberation and empowerment of an existence largely free from meaningless drudgery. But have we the collective wisdom and restraint to make it so? Or will the substitute for a viable market mechanism increasingly become brute force? How far would we have to go before those cut out of the social deck by this 'restructuring of work' will no longer accept their status peacefully? Do not the inner cities of some of our wealthiest societies suggest clearly enough what a people devoid of hope and purpose becomes?

My point here is to suggest that the traditional agendas of social purpose appear to offer little in the way of solutions to the effects of the technological imperative — nor any way of escape from them. Ironically, however, these agendas tend to elicit more and more fervent commitment to their particular rationales even as their ability to avoid a potentially catastrophic rupture of the social glue which holds us together becomes more and more tenuous. A commitment to an unbridled free-market, after all, will do nothing to alleviate the suffering of those for whom any possible work life has become an anachronism. Neither, however, will equalitarian moves toward a redistribution of wealth and income which undermines the incentive to invent and produce the high-tech products which have virtually become their own *raison d'être* and, in the process, an immensely powerful world economic engine.

Perhaps one ray of hope in the economic arguments is the need for demand if one is to realize a profit from supplying anything. Mass markets ultimately require mass consumption. Advertising can promote mass consumption (subject to various monetary control mechanisms) but it cannot sustain it in the absence of the means to purchase. The demand requirement, however, by no means suggests in and of itself, that a vast proportion of the population could not be entirely cut out of the process. All that is necessary is an increasing focus of productive capacity on big-ticket, 'top-end' products that are beyond the reach of any mass market.

In sum, recent exponential growth in high-technology knowledge and applications has left us in an unfamiliar social and economic world. On the one hand, technology is not optional. Those who cannot or will not use it to improve their efficiency and productivity will follow Darwin's less adaptive species. On the other, this very imperative sets us on a course toward a world in which only a tiny proportion of human talent, insight and ingenuity can be engaged in the production of consumer goods.

Worse still, in terms of immediate impacts on both rich and poor nations, the same efficiency logic drives multinational corporations concerned mainly about the bottom line at the highest corporate level to export the few remaining unskilled and minimally-skilled jobs (as well as particularly dangerous jobs and processes) to Third World nations where labour can be had for a fraction of its cost in developed countries. Thus jobs for the unskilled and minimally-skilled disappear completely from the developed nations at the same time that the economies of developing nations become more irreversibly tied to yesterday's jobs at bargain-basement wage levels. Can it be long, moreover, before even this last bastion of rote labour will be replaced by robotics?

Where will solutions come? Guaranteed annual incomes, work sharing, education for leisure? But what of merit, initiative and a sense of daily purpose and challenge? The answers to rethinking our sense of social purpose in light of the advent of high technology are far from obvious. We are left, however, with social and economic facts that can neither be ignored nor willed away. The potential impact on our ideas of schooling is every bit as great as on our ideas of what we ought to become as peoples and nations. With growing frequency, educational and training policies in many countries and jurisdictions have zeroed in on increasing support for learning in the high-tech fields, for education that supports and hastens the process of substituting capital and technology for human labour.

Environment

The technological revolution, of course, has occurred against a backdrop of mounting evidence that the price for it may be ecological apocalypse. The Minimata mercury-poisoning disaster was but the first of a series of major ecological disasters that persistently remind us of our vulnerability before the pollutants which our technologies produce so profusely. Evidence mounts that more than our lakes and rivers are in danger. The seas themselves, the principal source of the oxygen we breathe, appear equally in peril. 'The whales are dying' is becoming less a slogan of concern for endangered leviathan and more a cry of concern for what may soon happen — what may already be happening — to us. At least one of the world's great oceans has already lost its ability to support and give life. 'The Dead Sea' is no longer simply a term applied to a particular location of interest to biblical scholars. The Mediterranean is the first sea to have died in our time, but seems unlikely to be the last.

With the spectre of ecological apocalypse so persistently set before us by diverse pollution-induced disasters, and by those who study them, the attraction of a *laissez-faire* attitude toward the environment is less and less tenable even to the committed conservative ideologue. The principle of 'polluter pay', even to the extent of criminal liability for environmental damage, has become a respectable subject of political discussion even among those most deeply committed to the conservative social purpose agenda. In the schools, environmental awareness has generally escaped from its status as a closet curriculum offered by radically environmentalist teachers, to become part of the main-line curriculum. The critical long-term issue, of course, is the ultimate ability of technology to clean up its own mess. In one camp, the more evangelical environmentalists suggest that the problem is technology itself and that the only available escape from self-annihilation is retreat from the economic and technological growth imperatives, however impossible or unlikely such a retreat seems. In the other camp, the prophets of progress, generally much better financed and organized than their critics, reassure us that technology, directed by an enlightened self-interest which includes concern for environmental damage (especially where such public-spirited sentiment is encouraged by a polluter-pay principle that makes such damage a private cost) can rescue us from its own worst effects. Just who is right remains to be seen, but like death and taxes the subject is one of general interest and importance. Along with the fear of nuclear holocaust (perhaps somewhat blunted by recent East-West détente), the fear of ecological apocalypse, is very much part of the framework within which young people in our schools search for the meanings and possibilities of their existence.

Recreation and leisure have been hardly less radically altered than work by micro-electronics and other technologies. Television and video technology generally has invaded the home, if not replaced the hearth as its social centrepiece. For better or for worse, television now competes very favourably with schooling for the attention and loyalty of young persons. The video values of the sit-com, rock video and life-style commercials are, by any standard, profoundly different from those fostered by schooling in any traditional sense. For the most part, the content of our electronic media calls our young people not to the docility, reflection and long-term effort of the learner, but to the empty image, mindless action and instant gratification of soap-opera reality.

Television in its pop-entertainment dimension, moreover, has made a unique contribution to the devaluation of work outside senior business administration and the traditional professions. It has done so by its glamorization of and relatively exclusive attention to multi-national management, law, medicine and, to a much lesser extent, education. Intended or not, the bottom-line television-entertainment message to young people in many industrialized Western democracies is either that other occupations, except perhaps crime and law-enforcement, simply don't exist or that they are so hopelessly boring that the lives of those who work in them could never be interesting, much less 'entertaining'. It is surely no accident that the theme of youth indifference to preparing for the technological jobs that are available is a popular one among most Western governments (the Federal Republic of Germany with its unusually vital interface of private enterprise and public education being perhaps a notable exception).

In a more positive light, television has also become, for those who bother to watch news, cultural and documentary programs, a window on the world. Some, of course, would argue that this window is narrow, warped and given to the most unconscionable exploitation of human misery. But the global village bound together by electronic images is nonetheless now a reality in technologically advanced nations. The eye of the camera takes us in seconds from gas warfare in the Middle East to trapped whales in the Arctic. We are 'eye-witnesses' at the massacre of Tiananmen Square on the one hand and at the demolition of the Berlin Wall and all it stood for on the other. We have at our disposal a sense of electronically induced omniscience and omnipresence which can lead to both exhilaration and despair. Surely those who are the objects of our schooling efforts experience both, although one suspects a widespread preference among them for entertainment over information. If this is true, it may be because the kind of news they do see tends to inspire rather more of despair and fear than joy. It may also be that the sense of social purpose which the young of today acquire is jaded, as a result, with a new degree of cynicism and despair about the perfectibility, or even comprehensibility, of the human situation.

Women and Families

The feminist revolution of the last two decades has shaken our collective sense of who we are and what we should become every bit as deeply as snowballing technology. A sense of social purpose which little questioned that the proper place for most women was in the home has given way in most, though not all, industrialized nations to at least theoretical acceptance of, and support for, gender equity. While males and females remain eminently unequal in most measures of social status and economic power, not the least of which is responsibility for household chores, women have recently been written into social purpose agendas, that is, into our visions of what we would like to become, in a way that was simply unthinkable a decade-and-a-half ago. No longer do thoughtful males instinctively assume that women ought to be principally home-makers, child-bearers and women-behind-the-men of the workplace. A major change, forged in mutually painful confrontation, has emerged in our concept of gender and its meaning, and consequently in the place of women in our overall scheme of social purpose and becoming.

As in the case of rapid demographic change, only the Pacific-rim countries, notably Japan among industrial giants, have been isolated from the advance of feminist ideology. While an increasing number of Japanese women are taking courses at Special Training Colleges with a view toward pursuing a career rather than running a household (which is all the older Junior Colleges prepare women for), the current social reality there remains that of home-maker status for women and an almost exclusively male permanent workforce.[8]

Coincidentally with the rise of feminism and the sharp economic down-turn of the 1970s, the traditional nuclear family has lapsed into crisis in most industrialized nations. Up to half the children in some nations now find themselves in single-parent (and single income) homes, often cut off as well from the emotional and social support of an extended family. The turbulent lived reality of many such children — and potential consequences of this reality for school success — can hardly be over-estimated. As two senior administrative officials in Quebec recently put it:

A principal who searches his conscience in the matter ... [will find] that a young person who skips a class or fails an exam or a subject, is not responsible for what is happening ... [if] ... He no longer has the interior peace that makes study possible; [if] he lives in a universe of conflict the cause of which he cannot understand. He no longer has the support of a family framework and, without attempting to moralize, he is torn apart in his affective universe, in a world where values are fled and failure is denied.[9]

Children whose parents are not separated have within a very few years been transported from a world in which mother remained at home to one in which both parents work. Schools themselves have recently embraced a gender-egalitarian agenda by attacking sex-role stereotyping in their curricula, learning materials and language use, and thus increasingly support and help to legitimate changed feminine roles in the home, community and workplace. The broadened sense of individual purpose which feminism brought to women coupled with inflation and the consequent relative decline in the purchasing power of the traditional 'bread-winner's' income, as well as the progressive disappearance of whole categories of traditionally middle-class and lower-class jobs, has led the majority of women of child-bearing age into the workplace in Europe and North America. For better or for worse, and the debate continues on this issue, children whose pre-school learning and formation would have been largely in the hands of mothers a decade ago are now in day-care of some sort, or on a waiting list for day-care the supply of which seems every-where to lag far behind demand and need.

Secular Humanism and Christianity in the Schools

As the cultural make-up of nations and regions has become an ever-more kaleidoscopic mosaic, what little religious consensus may have once existed has largely disappeared. The history of some nations and regions, such as that of Holland or the Canadian province of New-foundland, necessitated confronting the challenges to public purpose and policy posed by religious diversity long before that necessity became clear in most Western democracies. Publicly funded schools in the United States, Australia and Canada have, in recent decades, lost their attachment to the pan-Protestant value and belief commitment from which (with the exception of religiously-affiliated separate but publicly funded and operated schools in some Canadian provinces) they sprang. In the view of many Christian parents such schools are adrift in a sea of secular humanistic moral relativism and have be-trayed their most fundamental mandate — moral formation of the young.

Demand for specifically denominational education, of course, is hardly new. The Catholic church has universally sought separate schooling arrangements for children of Catholic parents and has frequently pressed home its arguments for public funding of such schools.[10] What is new in Western industrial nations with a Christian heritage, is a growing alienation of traditional mainstream, and more recently fundamentalist, Protestant groups from public schools which members of such groups feel have sold out to the value-neutrality of secular humanism — or have become specifically and avowedly atheistic and amoral in the lived values and professed beliefs of their teaching personnel.

Obviously the nature of value alignments and commitments of public schools conceived within a common-school ethos had to change when the cultural commonality of their host societies dissolved. To adhere to pan-Protestant beliefs, moral prescriptions, Bible readings and explicitly Christian prayers would, over time, ensure the alienation and opposition of non-Christian parents whose numbers and electoral clout was and is rapidly growing. The nature of public schools in some Western democracies as *the Protestant public* system became untenable in culturally and religiously diverse, secular societies. As the last traces of the theocratic rationales for government gave way to purely secular views of social purpose, the public common school became, to the chagrin of many, the public secular school.

Alienation of many members of its traditional clientele has largely left common, 'publicly maintained' schools in the Western democracies struggling for a new sense of mission and purpose. Initially, that sense of purpose was conceived within a belief in the possibility of morally-neutral education. Increasingly, however, the possibility, in fact, the very meaning of such a belief, has come under heavy fire. As parents and policy-makers alike have zeroed in on the shaping of moral and belief commitments as the most essential part of the socialization mission of schooling, the question of what morals and belief commitments are to be fostered has dogged public school systems. The momentary refuge of values-identification and religious studies courses abstracted from any institutional commitment in these areas has been a fleeting one as parents ask more insistently what specific values and what specific beliefs public schooling stands for and fosters — and as parents, unhappy with the answers they receive or infer, move their children to private schools.

Thus demographic change is directly related to a renewed search for meaning, for a sense of moral purpose and direction, both in society and in its schools. At one level, our newfound cultural diversity suggests the need for many educations to serve many peoples. At another, however, it suggests that the common-school ideal may be more important than ever in cementing together a workable value consensus in society. Ultimately the question is whether the reality of cultural diversity is best served by structural pluralism — different institutions for different peoples — or by common institutions. Not long ago, the answer to this question seemed clear to most policy-makers. Today it is much less clear, especially in education. Just why this is so forms much of the substance of the next five chapters.

In Review

The rules of the social and educational policy games have changed profoundly in the last two decades. These changes, moreover, strike to the roots of our sense of who we are, and of what and who we can and should become. Our sense of cultural unity as peoples bound together by the political ties of the nation-state has largely disappeared except in countries that have escaped the direct effects of recent and massive population movements. Technology has changed irreversibly our conceptions of human capital, its development and its place in economic life. Increasingly, our ability to produce things depends less on humans, and on fewer humans, than ever before. The business, the agony, and only occasionally the ecstasy, of human existence in all corners of the earth is spread before us, 'live and in colour' every night.

Escape from the painful awareness of human misery has come in many forms — supercilious entertainment, drugs and alcohol among others. Such escapes from personal and vicarious pain, alienation and meaninglessness both shape and challenge our sense of social purpose. They equally shape and challenge our ideas about the limits and possibilities of schooling.

Notes

1 For a landmark study of this genre in education, one which virtually invented the lexicon of critical theory based on education as symbolic violence, see Pierre Bourdieu and Jean-Claude Passeron, *Reproduction In Education, Society and Culture*, trans. Richard Nice (London: Sage Publications, 1977).

2 For a careful and documented analysis of this process in OECD nations, see Stacy Churchill, *The Education of Linguistic and Cultural Minorities in the OECD Countries* (Clevedon: Multilingual Matters Ltd., 1986), especially pp. 33–60.

3 Stephen Heyneman of the World Bank has developed this theme in a number of places. Recently he did so in a presentation to the American Education Finance Association Annual Meeting. Stephen P. Heyneman, 'A look at the 1990s: Financing education a decade from now in develop-

ing countries' (paper delivered at the Annual Meeting of the American Education Finance Association, Tampa, Florida, 18 March 1988), p. 17.

4 While the agenda here is clearly to reverse the diminution and dilution of the French presence in Quebec, the result may be quite different since *all* Quebecois, not just those with French origins and home language, will be eligible for the new bonuses.

5 Joe Farrell, 'Cultural differences and curriculum inquiry', *Curriculum Inquiry*, 17 (1987), pp. 1–7.

6 Ira Shor, 'Equality is Excellence: Transforming teacher education and the learning process', *Harvard Educational Review*, 56 (November 1986), p. 407.

7 Charles Perrow, *Complex Organizations: A Critical Essay*, 3rd. ed. (New York: Random House, 1986), p. 270.

8 L. Cantor, 'The role of the private sector in vocational education and training: The case of Japan's special training schools', *The Vocational Aspect of Education*, 39 (1987), p. 36.

9 My translation of Vincent Tanguay and Bruno Giard, 'La qualité de l'enseignement ou l'éducation en évolution,' *Information*, 24 (November 1985), p. 41.

10 The United Kingdom, Ireland, New Zealand, Australia and the Netherlands, as well as several of the Canadian provinces, all have arrangements which permit public funds to be used in support of Catholic denominational schools.

Chapter 4

Frameworks for Understanding

A fundamental commitment to free-market ideology seems to imply a belief that private provision of schooling, like private provision of almost anything else, is inherently better than public provision. Whether public funding of education is appropriate and whether private schooling is a viable and meaningful concept where governments become heavily involved in funding 'independent' schools are separate, although important and closely related questions.

Conversely, commitment to equalitarian principles would seem to dictate a parallel commitment to large, centrally controlled school systems where resources are 'rationally' distributed according to some consistent and defensible equalization formula, and standardized and comparable educational outcomes are an important system objective. Of course, absolute commitment to ideological purity is at least as rare in educational policy as in the broader social policy arena. Few persons with a voice in educational policy matters are to be heard advocating either totally deregulated, privately delivered and financed schooling on the one hand, or centrally administered and controlled state schooling monoliths on the other. Most real-world politicians and educational policy thinkers find themselves walking a middle ground borrowing from each of the major competing ideologies and seeking to meld the results into something coherent and politically workable. Which side of that middle ground they walk, however, is very much a matter of their own personal inclination toward one of the major social policy agendas — and toward the beliefs on which they are founded.

Some Traditional Distinctions

In public finance and policy, the distinction between funding and delivery of services has been regarded as both fundamental and, until recently, robust. The justification for either or both public funding and public provision of a service was considered to lie in the inability or unwillingness of many persons or families to purchase a quantity and quality of a service believed desirable or necessary for all. Put otherwise, many 'goods', services and certain types of products intended for public use such as roads, were considered essential for the common welfare of the whole of society, even though, in some cases, they were addressed to or consumed by specific individuals and therefore provided a private benefit in addition to their public benefit. Although not without question, universal, compulsory schooling has long been regarded as just such a 'mixed good' required for the overall physical, social and economic well-being of societies at large, even though it is 'consumed' by individuals. Many economists have held that mixed goods should be provided in a mixed (partly public, partly private) market.[1] The widespread pattern of greater use of tuition and other user-pay fees to pass along more of the cost of education at the tertiary than at the secondary or elementary levels has arisen largely as a result of belief (buttressed by rate-of-return studies) that in education the greatest *private* good relative to public good arises at the tertiary level.

With two fundamental distinctions (public versus private funding and public versus private provision of services), four combinations are possible:

1   privately funded and delivered, the pure consumer or private good;
2   privately funded but publicly delivered, where consumer purchases from public agencies;
3   publicly funded but privately delivered, state service programs provided by local 'contractors'; and
4   publicly funded and delivered, state programs delivered by state agencies and paid for by public revenues.

These categories are not necessarily mutually exclusive. Some degree of 'user pay' (private funding) is not uncommon in services, such as water and sewer service, that are nonetheless provided by the government and heavily subsidized by tax revenues. The advent of compulsory and universal public education in the Western world at the end of the nineteenth century rapidly transformed schooling for most children in industrialized democracies from a privately provided and funded service — an object of free-market exchange — to one that was both publicly funded and provided. Only for those who could and did choose to send their children to private schools at a cost over and above their school tax burden did schooling remain, at least in part, a matter of free-market dynamics.

Provision of publicly funded services, however delivered, inevitably raises as an issue of public policy the question of their comparability across regions and among persons and groups. Both the equity of and access to such arrangements quickly become a matter of scrutiny and debate. *The decision to fund, and even more so to provide, a service publicly inescapably raises issues on the equalitarian social policy agenda,*[2] *issues which a completely private and deregulated sector avoids*. Indeed, the mere fact of public funding tends to invoke the whole range of concerns and proclivities in that agenda. When everyone's money is at stake, accountability and equity are perennial issues although the vocabulary, semantics and mathematics used to deal with them change with time and place.

In the broadest sense, no school is completely private or completely public. The most exclusive of private schools partake minimally — and often far more than minimally — of government largesse. Whether because of something as monetarily insignificant as access to publicly provided or subsidized learning materials or as significant as a major tax concession, private schools are always dependent to some degree on the operations and fiscal policies of government. Conversely, even in quite socialistic economies, schools must purchase some goods and services from private factor suppliers. At the very least, they must pay or otherwise compensate teachers. Despite such obvious impurities in the funding and delivery of schooling, the distinction between public and private schools was, and for the moment remains, a fairly robust one in most countries. The distinction, however, has become considerably more obscure at the post-secondary level in the post-war period as governments have heavily underwritten both operational and capital costs of universities and state vocational institutes. Increasingly, various levels of governments have come to contribute heavily to the operational budgets of *all* universities, including those that retain a 'private' legal status, doing so through both direct grants and research funds.

The old clear distinctions, however, are presently the subject of doubt and debate in certain countries, especially in regard to the wisdom of trying to maintain clear separation between the public and private sectors in education. Thus debate over how 'public' or 'private' the funding and provision of education ought to be has recently joined the more time-honoured debate over whether private or public education was better, and which mix of the two, if any, would be best at any particular educational level.

In the remainder of this chapter, I begin examining some basic forms of schooling in light of basic assumptions of the conservative, equalitarian and pluralist social purpose agendas. To do this, I consider the publicness or privateness of their funding and governance, as well as their ideological commitments and underpinning. I review the social policy and equity issues raised by varying approaches to schooling, focussing as I do so on underlying issues and agendas rather than on technical minutiae. In the process, I try to capture the significance for education of the changed public policy rulebook — the changed social and economic contexts — within which schooling in our time occurs. Finally, I present two frameworks for understanding schooling arrangements in different countries and regions.

The Abolition Option

No discussion of potential schooling arrangements would be complete without considering the possibility of doing away with schooling. However unrealistic, even weird, such a proposal may sound to most, champions of doing away with schools entirely — or of doing away with legal compulsion for all children to attend school — have not been wanting. Ivan Illich made the most celebrated, and perhaps the most optimistic, case for 'deschooling' society some two decades ago.[3] The root of Illich's argument was that, as presently conceived, schooling led to divisions and enmity within and among people. It also inevitably promoted — indeed was the most potent servant of — the 'Myth of Unending Consumption',[4] and hence *the* principle agent for ensuring the concerted and ongoing attention to mass production which he believed carried with it the inevitable price tag of ecological apocalypse. In his own words:

> Obligatory schooling inevitably polarizes a society; it also grades the nations of the world according to an international caste system. Countries are rated like castes whose educational dignity is determined by the average years of schooling of its citizens, a rating which is closely related to per capita gross national product, and much more painful.[5]

Schooling, Illich argued, does *not* promote common values,[6] does *not* bring about the self-perpetuating progress for all which it promises,[7] but *does* create a social myth of endlessly expanding need both for material goods and for more schooling.[8] While Illich set out many themes which radical critics of education would later write variations and amplifications of, he has clearly failed to convince policy-makers and their publics that doing away with schools — and, in particular, public schools — would be in the best interest of their societies. It seems certain that a complete demise of schooling would be vigorously opposed by business and industry in most countries and areas, partly for the reasons Illich advances, and partly for others. Perhaps more significantly, important internal contradictions exist in Illich's argumentation. If schools do not shape values powerfully, for instance, how can they be responsible for perpetrating and perpetuating the hoax of endless consumption in the minds of students? Moreover, the benefits Illich and others claimed for deschooling must now be considered from the vantage of many years of widespread experimentation and much disillusion with less directed and structured learning. Seen from such a perspective, Illich's optimism about the ability of technology to foster a society of voluntary learners bound together solely by shared interests and technology seems to strain even the most optimistic current visions of the power of technology in human learning. In its exuberance and self-assurance, that optimism surely rings hollow in this age of neo-conservative, if not reactionary, reconstructions of school curricula.

Despite the tenor of the times, however, certain champions of deschooling carry on the cause with such slogans as 'school is a place where children learn to be stupid' because 'others . . . take control of their minds' there.[9] While obviously framed within many of the basic assumptions of the conservative social policy agenda,[10] recent far-ranging criticisms of the quality and impact of public education in many lands have unanimously called for more, not less structure in schooling, for more, not less, time on the learning tasks of the schools, in short, for a general return to traditional basic subject content.[11] Current agendas of public and educational purpose, in short, cannot accommodate the idea of deschooling society. Even the most radical critics of education today speak not of deschooling but of radical schooling. We have lost whatever innocence, or naivete, once allowed us to flirt with the belief that a completely destructured learning environment could produce personal fulfilment and scholarship.

Short of the abolition of schooling but within a commitment to other ways of learning, there remains, of course, the possibility of simply abolishing the legal requirement for children to attend school. If compulsion were abolished, schools would serve only those who wanted to go, or whose parents wanted them to attend. While this might greatly ease the strain which the universal mandate of public schooling frequently places on public school personnel who cannot 'just say no' to students they would prefer to exclude (as private school administrators can), it would clearly fail to ensure some minimum quantity and quality of education for all. The argument for education as a public good, of course, suggests that such a minimum is necessary for our political and economic survival and well-being.

For would-be deschoolers there remains a less far-reaching option, home schooling, an option technically permitted under most existing public education legislation.[12] Almost invariably, however, the right to educate one's children at home is contingent upon inspection of the program of home study by public school officials who must determine that such instruction is within the minimum program demands set forth for that grade or level by state, provincial or regional authorities. While the right to home schooling has been claimed by some religious groups as an absolute right which the state cannot diminish or regulate, the reality of state regulation and approval has everywhere gone hand-in-hand with permission to educate children at home. To do otherwise, after all, would strike at the heart of compulsory attendance provisions in education legislation. Uninspected home schooling would be an automatic and universally available exemption from compulsory attendance.

The Traditional Private School

Much has been written about traditional 'elitist' private boarding schools along the lines of the British boys' school model, so much that a lengthy discussion here would only add to an information glut (although a very interesting one). In diverse lands such schools have had, and continue to have, social exclusivity as their principal objective and claim, although their claim to provide access and socialization to the 'best' (and most prosperous) group in society is always grounded in another claim, a claim to superior academic standards and, not infrequently, to a better fostering of rugged individualism through a rugged athletic regimen. In Cookston's terms, such schools fit Goffman's vision of total institutions,[13] institutions that control every aspects of their inmates' lives. They do so in order to launch

47

their students on a 'moral career' founded on commitment to and belief in being 'best' and, in doing so, they initiate students into a world view compatible with their probable future as leaders.[14] Such schools claim, above all, a unique and better moral formation than publicly operated and funded schools can offer.

Of course, the elite schools were by no means alone during the early evolution of formal schooling in the wake of the industrial revolution. The late eighteenth and the nineteenth century saw private grammar schools of different types and qualities arise in industrializing nations to provide education for children of the emerging middle class. Indeed, it was precisely because of the widely varying quality of these private but frequently not prestigious schools — and a widespread perception that the quality of many such schools was extremely low — that public financial support for private schools became public policy in most industrialized countries, and was, in turn, followed rapidly by establishment of publicly operated schools.

With the advent of public funding and provision of education, and legal compulsion to attend, social policy moves which occurred almost simultaneously in most of the industrialized nations of the Western world in the late nineteenth century, the elite schools found themselves once more virtually alone as providers of private education. Those who could afford to send their children to expensive and exclusive private schools and who wished their children to have access to the social and economic network such schools offered, did so. Those who could not, sent their children to public schools.

Only relatively recently have the high-prestige boarding schools, and their descendants and imitators, been joined by a wave of private schools responding to diverse motivations, commitments and clientelles. Private education is enjoying a growth internationally that ranges from modest but consistent to phenomenal. Part of the problem, of course, in assessing this growth is determining what private schooling is, and that increasingly difficult task is a major concern of much of what follows. Nonetheless, it is fair to say that privatization in all its guises is a very prominent feature of the evolution of schooling in our time. Nor is privatization a phenomenon isolated to a particular group of nations or peoples. It is eclectically international. That it should be so is fully consistent with the social purpose agendas of societies grown intensely wary of the ability of monolithic big-government social programs to deliver social cohesion, prosperity and public contentment. Education, after all, is far from alone among 'public goods' being handed over in a greater or lesser degree to the private sector. More and more of everything from public transportation to hospital care to postal service is being turned over to private initiative and entrepreneurship.

Private Schools, Public Schools: Archetypes and Hybrids

Before describing and analyzing the agendas and issues underlying various specific schooling alternatives, I wish to borrow gratefully a most useful conceptual framework for classifying private schools recently proposed by Daphne Johnson.[15] Johnson proposes a six-step 'philosophical continuum' of public policy for education, see figure 4.1. At one extreme of the continuum is the monolithic state system, a public monopoly completely financed out of the public purse, typically at the regional or national level. In such a system no parental choice is allowed beyond choices sanctioned within the state monopoly itself. Exit is impossible because the law allows no alternatives to the state system. Such Orwellian commitment to the principles of big-government equalitarianism in education has existed only in radically socialist states. Nonetheless, *the effect* of mixed private and public provision, of arrangements that allow both private and public schools can, at least for parents who cannot afford to exit from the state-supported system in their area, be much the same as such a state monopoly.

Johnson's second category is one step, although a very small one, in the direction of parental choice, allowing public and/or alternative denominational schools and school systems under one central public administration. Holland and the Canadian province of Newfoundland have educational policy frameworks that fit within this general rubric. Holland has, in fact, since enactment of the Dutch Constitution of 1917, sanctioned the division of all publicly provided services — in fact, almost all public activities — according to religion, and thus provides a clear example of a logic for public policy in general finding a close parallel in education. In Holland, health care, social services, media, political parties and trade unions are provided separately by and for each religious group, in a process known as *verzuiling* (columnization or pillarization).[16]

Johnson's 'competitive' framework involves the coexistence of publicly funded and provided schooling with completely privately funded and provided schooling. Choice is available for parents who wish, and can afford, it. Johnson's competitive/complementary framework is an example of mixed (public and private) provision of schooling viewed as a mixed good.[17] Not only are private schools

Figure 4.1 A philosophical continuum of schooling arrangements

Philosophical continuum	Collectivist					Individualist
Policy for public education	Monolithic state system of education	System of state education incorporating secular and religious	Public education freely available, meeting most/all educational needs. Individuals may 'opt out' and use independent institutions at their own expense. Central accreditation of these institutions, but no government support for such institutions or transactions.	Mixed economy of education (a combination of publicly and independently funded institutions) — Public education freely available, meeting most educational needs. Some government assistance enabling access to approved independent institutions	Free public education playing only a residual part in the combination (either low level education, or education focussed on deprived groups)	No publicly provided education. Public money funding educational 'vouchers' for families. Free market of independent educational institutions
	No opting out					
Column No.	1	2	3	4	5	6
Possible role for independent education	Non-existent		Competitive	Competitive/Complementary	Complementary	Universal
Implications for parental choice in education	No parental choice (except by moving house to change neighbourhoods)	Parental choice between secular and faith-linked institutions within the public system of education	Parental choice between public and independent education, but latter option must be fully backed by personal finance	Parental choice between public and independent education. Full economic cost of use of independent education not borne by family in all cases	Parental choice between public and independent education. Latter option needing to be backed by personal finance, except in selected means tested cases	Essential for parental choice to be exercised. Possibility of coupling personal finance to public money 'voucher'

Source: Johnson, D. (1987). *Private Schools and State Systems: Two Systems or One?* Philadelphia: Open University Press.

allowed to exist in direct competition with publicly-operated schools, some of the cost of 'private' education is payed out of the public purse. Johnson's next incremental step in public support for private education, the complementary framework, allows coexistence of public and private schools and requires personal payment for private school services, except where the parents of students who meet certain academic criteria are unable to pay private school tuition as determined by a standard test of their ability to pay (a 'means test'). In such cases, through one mechanism or another, some form of government tuition assistance is available.

Finally, in Johnson's 'universal' system we have the most completely publicly-funded-but-privately-provided option, a pseudo-private framework intended to simulate the advantages of free-market competition within a safety net of public funding, at least for those who need it. Vouchers, tax credits or direct grants, or combinations of these, underwrite more or less completely the operating and capital expenses of private schools. Public schools, as such, are disestablished, simply not provided for in law, and thus education becomes, at least formally, a creature of the market place and in-efficient and ineffective schools supposedly go the way of Darwin's less well-adapted species. Some, of course, argue that such a market would be anything but free, or that it places the principle of universal access to a basic-quality education at risk. Who, for instance, would want to establish schools in small and isolated centres where economic survival would be at best uncertain for very small private schools?

Champions of privatization, however, counter that the current mixed market in education, with a public sector inflated by its unique statutory status and assured access to vast public funding, undermines the principle of universal access to high-quality, or even minimum quality, education even more surely. Who has ever heard, they argue, of scholarships for children from low socio-economic-status neighbourhoods to attend an academically successful public high school in a rich neighbourhood. The most exclusive, class-stratified schools of all, such critics of public provision point out, are public schools in the 'right' neighbourhoods — not the 'elite' boarding schools and day schools.[18]

The more 'collectivist' of Johnson's frameworks coincide generally with the equalitarian agenda of social purpose.[19] Such frameworks view government provision and regulation as the route to protecting the educational consumer and the public in general. Standardization and equalization are by-words in a large bureaucratic system commissioned to meet all of everyone's needs equally. In the extreme case of the public monolith, the implicit *credo* is that bigger is better and the government knows best.

The opposite pole of Johnson's continuum, the individualist pole, however, is not congruent with the tenets of pure free-market ideology, although the types of arrangements it embraces are often touted as such. A pure free-market for mixed goods (those commonly believed to have benefits for the public even though they are privately 'consumed') would involve *both* the disestablishment of government provision *and* reliance on private financing — radical self-provision. Such an option appears nowhere on Johnson's continuum probably because, in its pure form, such a policy framework offends the sense of social justice of all but the most fanatically right-wing thinkers. Nonetheless, the surrogates for conservative ideology in Johnson's scheme are clearly the options at the 'individualist' (pseudo-private schooling market) end of her spectrum. Here, policy seeks to foster 'free' schools competing in an 'uncontrolled' market that does not pit them against a state-supported colossus — except that it is still government which funds most of the student spaces available in such schools. The dilemma of such a government-created 'free market' is that one is left with a probability approaching certainty of strong government regulation and control, of bureaucratized procedural requirements and legal definitions of program standards. Could any government which imposes on its people and enterprises the deadweight economic loss of taxes for mass provision of education (or any other service), truly 'deregulate' the market for that service? Put another way, can any government stay in power which allocates public funds without even the appearance of an accountability mechanism for them?

Despite such inescapable underlying political weaknesses, contradictions even, public funding with private provision becomes the educational policy agenda of many whose social purpose agenda is essentially *laissez-faire* capitalism. Since complete abandonment of government commitment to caring for those who cannot provide adequately for themselves is politically unacceptable, perhaps, after all, one can make the public sector work more like a free market. Advocates of the universalist schemes at the far-right of Johnson's spectrum contend that one *can* have the best of both worlds, on the one hand enough equalitarianism to 'ensure' some minimal degree of standardization at least of resource inputs (money, teacher qualifications, perhaps buildings, facilities etc.), and on the other, considerable competition-induced efficiency. Such, at least in democratic states, is the only politically tenable ground on which politicians of the right can defend free-market principles in basic areas of the social 'safety net', notably health, welfare and education.

To be sure, efforts to impose free-market principles and foster free-market dynamics in these policy domains vary greatly among governments. Some have, for instance, quite tenaciously preserved medical services as mainly a matter of both private provision and funding. In such jurisdictions, those who do not have the money (or insurance) for expensive surgical procedures become less and less likely to obtain them. Given the ballooning cost of heroic medical procedures and rapid graying of first world populations, moreover, even governments with strongly institutionalized commitments to universal and equally accessible health care have recently found them-selves groping for acceptable criteria to restrain access to very expen-sive medical services — and increasingly even to not so expensive services as well. Public resources, even in first world nations, after all, are not infinite; they are in fact scarce, and that is perhaps the most fundamental political fact confronted by all governments in good times and bad. Not all government spending can be consecrated to health care in the name of a right to heart transplants on demand, for instance. Neither can all government spending be consecrated to education which provides each child with a private tutor on demand. Especially hard choices loom before the governments of ageing populations, and schooling will almost certainly become less and less its own justification as governments are forced to make these choices.

Figures 4.2 and 4.3 show an alternative, more comprehensive conceptual scheme for classifying schooling arrangements. The ulti-mate publicness or privateness of schooling arrangements can be con-sidered a result of three elements:

1   provision, that is, how public or private is the governance of the institutions providing education;
2   the mix of public and private funding; and
3   the degree of government regulation of public and private education.

In some respects, of course, these distinctions are analytic, that is, the three categories are dependent on one another. Nonetheless, this framework has the advantage of making explicit the public/private funding and provision dimensions on the one hand, and of separating them from the degree of government regulation on the other.[20] Such a separation is admittedly partly artificial. Much of the weight of the public and educational finance literature, after all, is arrayed in favour

Figure 4.2   The three dimensions of publicness/privateness

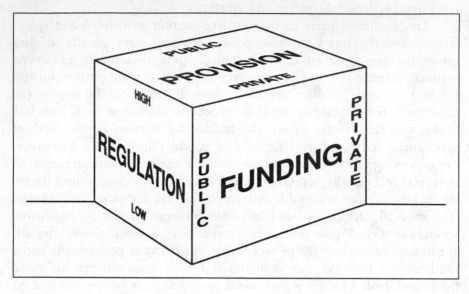

Figure 4.3   The two bipolar extremes of publicness and privateness

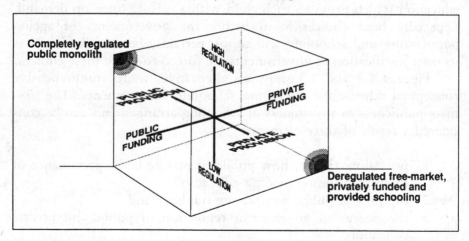

of the belief that public funding automatically brings government regulation of program and governance as well as of fiscal affairs. An arrangement with, say, high levels of public funding and a local autonomy approaching independence would seem, therefore, highly unlikely. Nonetheless, for comprehensiveness, the framework laid out in figures 4.2 to 4.5 includes politically unlikely, although theoretically possible, arrangements for education, arrangements such as the

Figure 4.4   Funding and provision options at a high level of regulation

Private ◀————— **PROVISION*** —————▶ Public

FUNDING	Private				Public
Private	1. Tightly regulated but nominally independent schools. Parents who can afford schooling have a choice of where to send children but little say in program, value formation, etc.	2. Tightly regulated mainly independent schools, although some schools or programs are operated by government on a user-pay basis. Parents who can afford schooling can choose schools but not program content and value orientation.	3. Tightly regulated mixed arena in which government provides some schools or programs but all schooling is on a user-pay basis. Parents who can afford schooling can choose schools but not program content and value orientation.	4. Tightly regulated mainly government provided schooling but available only on a user-pay basis. Parents who can afford schooling can choose schools but not program content and value orientation.	5. Tightly regulated government monopoly on the provision of schooling but available only on a user-pay basis. Parents who can afford schooling can choose schools but not program and value orientation.
	6. Tightly regulated but nominally independent schools. Some government funding, which gives more parents the option to choose to buy schooling but little say in program, values, etc. ■ If 'full' government funding is available for all students unable to pay fees, then all parents have this choice.	7. Tightly regulated mainly independent schools although some schools are operated by government. Some government funding, which gives more parents the option to choose to buy schooling but little say in program, values, etc. ■ If 'full' government funding is available for all students unable to pay fees, then all parents have this choice.	8. Tightly regulated mixed arena in which government provides some schools or programs. Some government funding, which gives more parents the option to buy schooling but little say in program, values, etc. ■ If 'full' government funding is available for all students unable to pay fees, then all parents have this choice.	9. Tightly regulated mainly government provided schooling. Some government funding, which gives more parents the option to choose to buy schooling but little say in program, values, etc. ■ If 'full' government funding is available for all students unable to pay fees, then all parents have this choice.	10. Tightly regulated government monopoly on the provision of schooling. Some government funding, which gives more parents the option to choose to buy schooling but little say in program, values, etc. ■ If 'full' government funding is available for all students unable to pay fees, then all parents have this choice.
Public	11. Tightly regulated publicly funded but nominally independent schools. All parents may choose school but have little say in program, values, etc.	12. Tightly regulated publicly funded mainly independent schools although some schools are operated by government. All parents may choose school but have little say in programming, values, etc.	13. Tightly regulated publicly funded mixed arena in which government provides some schools or programs. All parents may choose school but have little say in programming, values, etc.	14. Tightly regulated publicly funded mainly government provided schooling. All parents may choose school but have little say in programming, values, etc.	15. Tightly regulated publicly funded government monopoly. The public monolith under tight central control. All parents may choose school but have little say in programming, values, etc.

* The publicness or privateness of provision, as Pring (1987) points out, involves much more than public or private schools and educational programs. For simplicity sake, the chart distinguishes only in terms of whole schools and programs, but the provision may vary as well by which specific goods and services are purchases from which sector (e.g., books from private sector and computer services or supervision from public sector).

■ Indicates universal, compulsory education is a possibility.

Figure 4.5 *Funding and provision at a low level of regulation*

PROVISION* (Private → Public), FUNDING (Private → Public)

	Private →				→ Public
Private ↓ FUNDING	16. Autonomous private schools, the pure free-market option. Parents who can afford schooling send children to school according to program and value preferences.	17. Autonomous private schools and some government-provided schools and programs. All schools are on a user-pay basis. Parents who can afford schooling send children to school according to program and value preferences.	18. Deregulated mixed arena in which government provides some schools or programs but all schooling is on a user-pay basis. Parents who can afford schooling send children to school according to program and value preferences.	19. Deregulated mainly government-provided schooling but available only on a user-pay basis. Parents who can afford schooling send children to school according to program and value preferences.	20. Deregulated government monopoly on schooling but all schooling is user-pay. Parents who can afford schooling send children to school according to program and value preferences.
	21. Autonomous private schools but partial government funding which gives more parents the option to buy schooling and choose from schools with different programs and value orientations. ■ If 'full' government funding is available for all students unable to pay fees, then all parents have this choice.	22. Autonomous private schools and some government-provided schools and programs. Partial government funding gives more parents the option to buy schooling and choose from schools with different programs and value orientations. ■ If 'full' government funding is available for all students unable to pay fees, then all parents have this choice.	23. Deregulated mixed arena in which government provides some schools or some programs. Partial government funding gives more parents the option to buy schoolings and choose from schools with different programs and value orientations. ■ If 'full' government funding is available for all students unable to pay fees, then all parents have this choice.	24. Deregulated mainly government provided schooling. Partial government funding gives more parents the option to buy schooling and choose from schools with different programs and value orientations. ■ If 'full' government funding is available for all students unable to pay fees, then all parents have this choice.	25. Deregulated government monopoly on schooling. Partial government funding gives more parents the option to buy schooling and choose from schools with different programs and value orientations. ■ If 'full' government funding is available for all students unable to pay fees, then all parents have this choice.
↓ Public	26. 'Autonomous' private schools but completely publicly funded. All parents may choose schools and choose from schools with different programs and value orientations.	27. 'Autonomous' private schools and some government-provided schools and programs. All parents may choose schools and choose from schools with different programs and value orientations.	28. Deregulated mixed arena in which government provides some schools and programs. All parents may choose schools and programs.	29. Deregulated mainly government-provided schooling. All parents may choose schools and choose from schools with different programs and value orientations.	30. Deregulated government monopoly on schooling, the ultimately unaccountable bureaucratic nightmare. All parents may choose schools and choose from schools with different programs and value orientations such schools might have.

* The publicness or privateness of provision, as Pring (1987) points out, involves much more than public or private schools and educational programs. For simplicity sake, the chart distinguishes only in terms of whole schools and programs, but the provision may vary as well by which specific goods and services are purchases from which sector (e.g., books from private sector and computer services or supervision from public sector).

■ Indicates universal, compulsory education is a possibility.

completely private, deregulated, free-market option, which Johnson's scheme overlooks.

Figures 4.4 and 4.5 present descriptions of the kind of schooling arrangements and parental choice which varying mixes of public and private provision and funding result in at the two extremes of the regulation dimension. Figure 4.4 displays arrangements and choices available in a regime of intense and far-reaching government regulation of education. Figure 4.5 explores the arrangements and resulting choices at the opposite end of the regulation spectrum, that is, completely unregulated schooling.

Figure 4.4 shows that in a tightly regulated educational arena, completely private funding (options 1 to 5) might underwrite different mixes of public and private provision but would offer little parental choice among competing programs and value orientations. Moreover, since all schooling in options 1 to 5 is paid for from private resources, only those who can afford to send their children to a particular school (private or government) will be able to do so. Since both sectors are intensely regulated, little freedom to vary program and value orientations exists. The likelihood of a private educational sector emerging and sustaining itself in a regime of rigid government control is, of course, highly doubtful. Without the power to be, or at least appear, different in program or value commitments, private schools would be highly unlikely to muster the necessary client support and entrepreneurial vigour to survive. Moreover, the political will to enforce strong regulation on an activity completely financed by private funding would be the product of a truly bizarre combination of Conservative and equalitarian beliefs.[21] Options 1 to 5, if interesting, are therefore probably hypothetical categories. They, like several other options in the framework as a whole, however, contribute to an instructive gestalt of possibility.

Options 6 to 10 of figure 4.4 set out probable arrangements and parental choice in a mixed funding regime within a context of pervasive government control of program and governance. Again, variations of the provision mix would offer little change in a parental choice still limited to choosing from among schools that offer essentially identical programs and value orientations (a condition imposed by the high-regulation assumption). More parents, however, would be able to make this choice, limited as it would be. In fact, if government funding were available for all students, then all parents could choose a school (if, of course, that choice were not itself regulated). Universal attendance becomes a possibility only with a commitment to universal public funding — at least for those who could not otherwise afford a basic-quality education. An absolutely crucial question in assessing the degree of school choice available to all parents is whether tight regulation includes, on the one hand, setting limits to fees charged by private and/or public schools, and, on the other, controlling or outlawing the ability of schools to admit pupils selectively. Since this is a maximum regulation paradigm, I have assumed that private school fees are controlled and that access is a function of supply and ability to pay only. Options 6 to 10 are at least theoretically conceivable either within a regime of government subsidies aimed at making schooling available to more, but not all parents, or a regime aimed at sending every child to a school.

Options 11 to 15 of figure 4.4 re-emphasize that universality and hence compulsory education is only conceivable where full government funding is at least available for all students who may need it. The difference from the options 6 to 10 is that *all* funding passes through government in such arrangements. In options 11 to 15, all parents may choose a school, but once again since all schools offer the same thing that choice largely lacks substance. The key question about the choice offered in these options (as in those of options 6 to 10) is whether full public funding is available for *all* students who require it.[22] If universal funding is available, universal attendance is at least a possibility and compulsion to attend is not an overt contradiction in policy. What figure 4.4, as a whole, points to most forcefully is that some freedom from the strictures of regulation is a necessary, but not sufficient, condition for meaningful parental choice among different educational programmes and value and belief commitments.

Options 16 to 20 of figure 4.5 lay out the consequences of various mixes of public and private schooling in a completely deregulated market with no public funding. These range from the complete free-market option (option 16) to the unlikely situation of a government-run monopoly accessible only and completely on a fee-for-service basis. Since access to schooling in any of options 16 to 20 is strictly determined by ability to pay, parents may, if they choose, send their children to whatever school they wish and can afford. Furthermore, since the market is unregulated much diversity can be expected among school programs and value orientations. Thus the choice of parents who can afford to choose will be substantial and consequential both in terms of learning outcomes and the moral formation of their children. They will exercise that choice, however, in a market whose only safeguard is 'buyer beware'. Those who cannot afford education, of course, would not get it in options 16 to 20.

Typically the mixing of public and private funding has meant that public schools were predominantly publicly funded and private schools were predominantly privately funded but that equation is rapidly eroding in certain countries and regions. Options 21 to 25 of the deregulated paradigm shows the results of mixed funding across various mixes of private and public provision. As in mixed-funding arrangements at any level of regulation, choice is available only to some parents unless complete government funding is available to all who could not otherwise pay. The choice throughout the deregulated paradigm, however, will be much more than just a school building.

Options 26 to 30 lay out the possibilities for completely public funding in a deregulated environment, surely most unlikely arrangements all. At one extreme (option 26, the pseudo free-market option), all schooling would be provided by nominally autonomous private schools receiving some sort of unaccountable block funding or competing for educational vouchers (certificates provided by governments to parents and redeemable for the purchase of educational services) with no government strings attached. At the other extreme (option 30) looms the ultimate bureaucratic nightmare, a completely deregulated state monopoly, in short, a state organ given the exclusive right to provide service in a major market sector (education being largest single employer in many advanced countries) with no attempt to limit or define the nature and process of the schooling it provides.

In societies unwilling to commit to exclusively conservative or equalitarian purpose agendas with their all-or-nothing views of government regulation,[23] some middle-ground approach to the regulation of schooling inevitably develops. In the end, the most interesting and controversial combinations, as well as the most politically tenable, lie in this middle zone of moderate regulation. Most real-world schooling arrangements, moreover, have different degrees of regulation for publicly operated schools than for privately operated schools. As well, the proportion of revenues deriving from government sources for any school or type of school is often closely related to regulation. Partly because of the difficulties and ambiguities of this central zone, and partly because I believe anyone interested in exploring the power of this model should work through one regulation paradigm alone, I leave the all important middle ground for the reader to explore. I will later argue that middle solutions (in terms of provision and funding as well as regulation) are increasingly the only politically sustainable ones.

Educational resources insufficient to meet even the most minimal needs of all or most children is a reality confronted by many heavily indebted Third World governments and, whatever the degree of regulation, such governments must severely limit the number of places available even for the most basic education. One of the primary pieces of advice currently being offered to such nations by the World Bank is precisely that they privatize their educational system in the name of concentrating on quality rather than quantity in educational matters (not to mention trimming government expenditures which sap the ability of such countries to service their debts).[24] Such advice, of course, is often not taken in under-developed countries at the receiving end of the transfer by multinational corporations of remaining menial and dangerous work since it is, not coincidentally, in just such countries that rate-of-return studies on educational investment show consistently highest return at the lowest educational levels.[25] Moreover, since the economic crunch of the mid-1970s, even relatively wealthy nations have had to reconsider critically the meaning, costs and benefits of educational universality. Most continue to do so with some vigour.

Finally, both the Johnson framework[26] and my own can easily be applied to mixed-good markets other than education. Although it appears unlikely at first glance, even social welfare can be viewed usefully and critically in terms of Johnson's spectrum and of the three dimensions of provision, funding and regulation. Surely health care fits both models. Active experimentation is underway in many countries with various mixes of regulation, provision and funding for health services. Whatever mixed good one considers, *choices among possible role relationships of the private and public sectors in delivering that service, as well as related funding and regulation choices, will ultimately hinge on evolving commitment to competing visions of social purpose, to our sense, that is, of who we are and ought to become as peoples and nations.*

Alternatives and Choices

Choice is the bedrock issue of social and economic policy and hence, not surprisingly, of education. What choices, by whom and with what restraints are the stuff of political debate everywhere. The argument for combined public and private activity in mixed-good fields is primarily founded on providing maximum choice within necessary constraints and safeguards. Most people want, for instance, a choice of doctors, hopefully even of treatment programs, but not the choice to unwittingly commit one's survival to a quack. One wants to preserve parental choice in the selection of the educational program and schooling environment of children. Such choice has, in fact, been advanced as a basic human right by the United Nations. Section 3 of Article 26 of the *Universal Declaration of Human Rights* states that 'Parents have a prior right to choose the kind of education that shall be given to their children'. Yet the public value of a mixed good such as education can be greatly diminished if educational charlatans are allowed to sell their wares unhindered — and even at public expense. On the other hand, proponents of more freedom in the educational marketplace frequently argue that it is precisely public provision and regulation which, by sheltering incompetence, provides the most fertile ground for educational charlatanism, not private provision and deregulation.[27]

Tiebout argued that choice is eminently possible with public provision and funding.[28] Families exercise choice about all manner of mixed goods from parks and golf-courses to schools, he believed, by moving to neighbourhoods where their own preference for such goods are most closely met. Those who like beautiful golf courses gravitate to neighbourhoods whose municipal governments provide them, while those who prefer expensive schools go to neighbourhoods with expensive schools. Thus, Tiebout argued, the public sector mimics the private with migration rather than direct purchase as the measure of utility and demand. Unfortunately, Tiebout overlooked the fact that large segments of national populations, by virtue of limited income and wealth, lack the ability to express their preferences for mixed goods by moving. A poor family is unlikely, in any nation, to have the option of moving to a neighbourhood with either good golf courses or good schools. And even if all families were able to move at will according to their preferences, the question of differences in access to information would linger. Considerable evidence, for instance, suggests that higher socioeconomic-status parents have greater access than others to 'better' information about all mixed goods, including schools, and would therefore select schools and programs more likely to produce better life outcomes for their children, even if mobility could somehow be equalized.[29]

Finally, all of the discussion and analysis of this chapter can be applied to schooling *at all levels*. The mix of provision, funding and regulation at different levels, however, will vary based on beliefs about the nature of the private versus public benefits conferred by schooling *at that level* as well as on perceptions of the general economic and social utility of broad access to education at that level.

Post-secondary education, for instance, is commonly believed to have a greater private benefit component than elementary education and is therefore rarely completely supported out of public funds.

Conclusion

The arrangements we make for schooling are ultimately products of our vision of what the good society is and how we might and can move in that direction. Depending on those beliefs — and such beliefs tend to group themselves in a general way into the agendas of *laissez-faire* capitalism, equalitarianism and structural pluralism — we prefer schools, as well as other mixed good institutions, which are more or less publicly funded, more or less publicly provided and more or less tightly bound by government regulation. Rejecting, as I believe we must, the option of deschooling our societies, we are left to ponder the basic options before us in the way governments can mix the educational market. The question is not whether to school, but how, at whose cost, for whose benefit and under whose control.

The following chapter looks at current types of schooling arrangements in light of the two frameworks presented here, especially the latter. In it, I examine systematically the rationales advanced by proponents and critics of each basic approach to the provision of schooling. I conclude with a review of directions and trends in such arrangements.

Notes

1   See, for instance, Richard A. Musgrave and Peggy B. Musgrave, *Public Finance in Theory and Practice* (New York: McGraw-Hill Book Co., 1980), p. 79.
2   See p. 15.
3   Ivan Illich, *Deschooling Society* (New York: Harper and Row, 1971), pp. 9–24.
4   *Ibid.*, p. 38.
5   *Ibid.*, p. 9.
6   *Ibid.*, pp. 38–40.
7   *Ibid.*, pp. 42–3.
8   *Ibid.*, p. 44.
9   John Holt, *Teaching Your Own: A Hopeful Path for Education* (New York: Delacorte Press/Seymour Lawrence Book, 1981), p. 231.
10 See p. 8.

11 For two among many examples of such criticisms, see The National Commission on Excellence in Education, *A Nation at Risk* (Cambridge, Mass.: USA Research, 1984), pp. 5–14; and George Radwanski, *Ontario Study of the Relevance of Education, and the Issue of Dropouts*, (Toronto: Ontario Ministry of Education, 1987), pp. 25–64.

12 Among North American jurisdictions only Kansas and Texas refuse absolutely to recognize home instruction, see Patricia M. Lines, 'The new private schools and their historic purpose,' *Phi Delta Kappan*, 67 (January 1986) p. 378.

13 Erving Goffman, *Asylums* (Chicago: Aldine Publishing, 1961), pp. 3–124.

14 Peter W. Cookson, Jr., 'Boarding schools and the moral community', *The Journal of Educational Thought*, 16 (August 1982) pp. 90–2.

15 Daphne Johnson, *Private Schools and State Systems: Two Systems or One?* (Philadelphia: Open University Press, 1987), p. 7.

16 E. James, 'Benefits and costs of privatized public services: Lessons from the Dutch educational system', *Comparative Education Review*, 28 (November 1984), p. 607.

17 See p. 43.

18 D. Doyle, 'A din of inequity: Private schools reconsidered', *Teachers College Record*, 82 (Summer 1981), p. 667.

19 See p. 15.

20 Even this scheme is a simplification in that it does not make explicit the important distinction between regulation of public and regulation of private schools.

21 See pp. 8 and 15.

22 No logical necessity, of course, compels this assumption. One could have a completely publicly-funded system with a supply of school places smaller than the number of potential students for such places and simply allow part of the demand for schooling to remain unmet. Such is precisely the situation in many third-world countries.

23 See pp. 8 and 15.

24 Stephen Heyneman of the World Bank explained this position and the rationale behind it in a presentation to a recent American Education Finance Association Annual Meeting, see Stephen P. Heyneman, 'A look at the 1990s: Financing education a decade from now in developing countries' (Paper delivered at the Annual Meeting of the American Education Finance Association, Tampa, Florida, 18 March 1988).

25 See, for instance, Donald Richards and Eugene Ratsoy, *Introduction to the Economics of Canadian Education* (Calgary: Detselig Enterprises Ltd., 1987), pp. 71–2.

26 See p. 49 and Figure 4.1.

27 See, for instance, William Burt, 'The new campaign for tax credits: "Parochiaid" misses the point', in *Family Choice in Schooling*, ed. Michael Manley-Casimir (Toronto: D.C. Heath and Company, 1981), p. 154.

28 For a succinct summary of Tiebout's consumer choice model of public services, see Charles Benson, *The Economics of Public Education*, 2nd. ed. (Boston: Houghton Mifflin, 1968), p. 131. For the original statement, see Charles M. Tiebout, 'A pure theory of local expenditures', *Journal of Political Economy*, 64 (October 1956), pp. 416–24.

29 See, for instance, William Garner and Jean Hannaway, 'Private schools: The client connection', in *Family Choice in Schooling*, ed. Michael Manley-Casimir (Toronto: D.C. Heath and Company, 1981), p. 127; or Michael A. Olivas, 'Information inequities: A fatal flaw in parochiaid plans', in *Private Schools and the Public Good: Policy Alternatives for the Eighties*, ed. Edward M. Gaffney (Notre Dame: University of Notre Dame Press, 1981), p. 138.

Chapter 5

Options and Alternatives

A wide range of alternatives are currently being used, implemented and considered across the Western world today for melding private and public provision of education. I deal with them in the order suggested by the framework for understanding I proposed in the previous chapter. Specifically, I work from the most to the least public in terms of provision and funding and in decreasing order of regulation. Finally, I situate these alternatives within the tenets of conservative and equalitarian ideologies.[1] I make no claim to exhaustiveness, although I believe that this and the following chapter provide a thorough look at basic types of schooling arrangements being used and considered internationally.

The Common School Centerpiece Model

The most public schooling markets are those with the greatest proportion of government provision, funding and regulation — in the extreme case, Johnson's 'monolithic state system of education.'[2] A state monopoly on schooling can, in theory, exist at any level of regulation and with any combination of funding. In reality, however, attempting to regulate finely every detail of organizational operation is self-defeating. Therefore, the highly regulated options in figure 4.4, p. 55 should be considered as occurring at a maximum feasible level of control, rather than as some imaginary state of absolute central hegemony over every detail of organizational life. The result of excessive central control efforts more often lead to no control than perfect control. Similarly, the only practical way to eliminate all private schooling is to proscribe it specifically by law. Referring to figure 4.4, options 5, 10 and 15 are therefore available only when the state forbids all private schooling, a tack possible only within the extreme equalitarianism of doctrinaire socialism. Options 1 to 5 in figure 4.4, moreover, are improbable, although not unheard of, because private consumption, funding and provision are rarely compatible with tight government regulation. The sale of alcoholic beverages in countries without state vending agencies, however, is a good example of an enterprise that often is tightly controlled by government regulations but is, nonetheless, largely a matter of private exchange. Such activity illustrates that the first five options figure 4.4, while rare, are not a null set. Nonetheless, I know of no jurisdiction where schooling is exclusively privately funded yet tightly regulated.

In economies not forged specifically from a radically socialist agenda, therefore, the most public educational arenas possible are those with large, nominally homogeneous state school systems that enrol the vast majority of students at a given educational level and purport to provide equal educational treatment and opportunity for all. Within a remarkably short period after the more-or-less simultaneous inception of universal, compulsory schooling in most Western industrialized nations during the late nineteenth century, the large, near-monopolistic, publicly funded, publicly administered school system had become a common, though by no means unique, model of schooling. First, at the elementary level, finally at the secondary level, but never really at the post-secondary level, the idea of free, and therefore formally equal, access to publicly maintained schooling became a dominant goal of social and educational planning in many countries. It became so wherever governments committed themselves to more equalitarian social purpose agendas — and were convinced of the contribution of education to economic productivity and the common good.

The evolution of mass public education at the primary and secondary level appears to have been most successful in the presence of relative religious homogeneity — or of pervasive secularization. Estelle James's recent work strongly suggests the central role that religious, and deep-seated cultural and linguistic, cleavages have played in fostering deviations from the near public-monolith model suggested most clearly by option 9 and, although much less likely politically, by option 10, the public-monopoly option, in figure 4.4.[3] Specifically, in jurisdictions where considerable cultural and religious homogeneity existed, the common school became, *and survived as*, both an important object and instrument of social policy. Where, as in the United States, relative religious homogeneity was supplanted by a strong and pervasive commitment to secular views of social purpose,

---

The Common School Centrepiece

Provision: Mainly public. Most pupils in public schools but private schools allowed.
Funding: Public for public schools and private for private schools.
Regulation: Moderate to high for public schools. Varies for private schools but tends
   to be light.

For the Conservative Agenda:
   +   Allows private schools to exist and imposes a minimum of regulation on them.
   −   Creates a huge publicly operated public system and therefore offends principles
       of minimal government interference in marketplace and selfprovision.
For the Equalitarian Agenda:
   +   Creates a close-to-universal publicly supported and operated school system and
       makes possible fiscal and educational equalization efforts.
   −   Allows private schools to exist and to do so with little or no government
       regulation.

---

the common, school ideal survived, more or less intact, the relatively gradual demographic changes of the early twentieth century.

With the common school inevitably comes the question of a common curriculum. That question has two primary dimensions: *how much* of the curriculum should be shared as a common core among *all* students (except, perhaps, those with severe learning disabilities), and *how long* should most of the curriculum be shared before students move off on different learning paths. Answers to these question have varied in different countries and times. The common-school centre-piece may, in fact, only involve students in a shared core of learning experiences for a very few years of primary education — or it may extend, as many advocates of a common curriculum in the United States and Great Britain currently advocate, over most of the primary and secondary years of schooling. The essence of the common-school ideal, however, rests not upon all students doing the same things and learning the same material, but rather on all students, or at least the overwhelming majority, sharing some aspects of their school experi-ence; at the very least, attendance at shared school facilities that are similar in some significant way (usually in the range of learning opportunities offered there). Whether such universally shared experi-ence is a good thing or not, of course, depends on one's beliefs about the value of funnelling all young people through a more or less common schooling process, and opinion is increasingly divided about this.

In this broad sense, great differences exist in the degree to which countries can be said to have a common-school centrepiece arena for schooling, and at what educational levels. In the United States, for

67

instance, with 85 per cent of students in state-run, public primary and secondary schools, most students can, in one sense at least, be said to share in a common public-school experience.[4] Nonetheless, the process and content of the education a student experiences in an inner-city Detroit public high school is, from all evidence, different in almost every conceivable particular, from the those which a student in, say, up-state New York or Beverly Hills experiences. Indeed, the argument is often put forward that the 'most exclusive' schools are not élitist private schools with big-ticket price tags (at least they provide some scholarships based on merit and need) but public schools in the 'right' neighbourhoods (to which no scholarships are ever provided). Moreover, the streaming of students into different 'ability' tracks is a ubiquitous practice in American education and further differentiates the schooling experience of students in the American 'common' public schools. In Germany, despite one common public-school system which captures 90 per cent of the student population,[5] students are segregated into radically different educational streams quite early in their school careers, although recent reforms have made the segregation into academic (*Gymnasium*) and non-academic streams (*Hauptschule* and *Realschule*) somewhat later and less final than in the past.[6] As is the case in most European countries, a much smaller proportion of the population than in the United States or Canada remains in school to the end of secondary and into post-secondary education. All this complicates the issue of how much is common to the 'common-school' experience of pupils.

The equalitarian ethos, in any case, carries within its demands for equalization and standardization a mandate for standardizing the education that all children receive. The issue of whether, and to what degree, schools should offer all students a relatively consistent gestalt of educational programming is never far below the surface of educational policy discussion in countries and regions with large, state-run and supported public school systems. All working compromises on common content and process in schooling depend ultimately on the sense of social purpose shared by members of a society able to influence public policy at any given moment. The relationship between social purpose agendas and educational policy, however, as figure 5.1 suggests, is always complex and not infrequently paradoxical.

To simplify greatly, as the values of those who shape educational policy leans in the direction of a conservative social purpose agenda, the primary emphasis in educational policy would logically tend to shift toward the *classic educationally progressive ideal* of different kinds of education for different kinds of students — that is, toward different

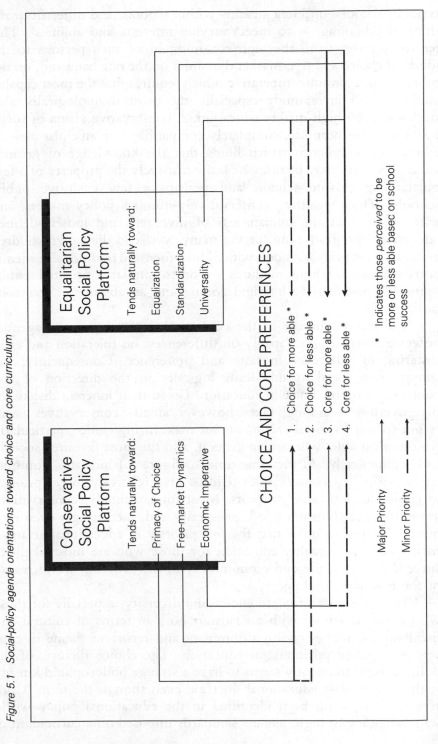

Figure 5.1   Social-policy agenda orientations toward choice and core curriculum

Conservative
Social Policy
Platform

Tends naturally toward:

Primacy of Choice

Free-market Dynamics

Economic Imperative

Equalitarian
Social Policy
Platform

Tends naturally toward:

Equalization

Standardization

Universality

CHOICE AND CORE PREFERENCES

1. Choice for more able *
2. Choice for less able *
3. Core for more able *
4. Core for less able *

*   Indicates those *perceived* to be
    more or less able based on school
    success

Major Priority

Minor Priority

types of schools, different streams within schools, and different quantities of schooling — to meet 'varying interests and abilities'. This tendency arises from the high commitment of such persons to the ideals of choice and free-market dynamics on the one hand and, on the other, to an economic imperative which requires that the most capable students, and increasingly especially the most technologically able students, get a high-quality education. A conservative vision of social purpose is, furthermore, completely compatible with an élitist view of educational excellence which holds that the knowledge of greatest value to society may be more or less exclusively the property of a few outstanding private schools and perhaps a few exclusive public schools. Thus wealthy, conservatively-minded policy-makers and parents can tout the humaneness of divergent and loosely-defined educational programming for the many, yet send their own children either to élitist private schools with tightly-focussed traditional academic curricula and teaching methods — or to similarly oriented public schools kept exclusive by rigid zoning and an absence of interzone busing.

The ethos inherent in the conservative social purpose agenda, however, focusses inescapably on differences: on toleration and even fostering of difference in taste and preference. Consequently, the conservative social agenda leads logically in the direction of less control and more choice in education. Given their inherent dislike for big government and high taxes, however, small-c conservatives usually put forward various arguments for maximizing choice, particularly for the most able, who are, in general, also the most favoured socially and economically. At the same time, as figure 5.1 indicates, committed social policy conservatives tend to give relatively lower priority to choice for less 'able' students. Most fundamentally, conservatives argue that the common good, prosperity and, increasingly even economic survival, require that the *first* priority in educational arrangements be a high-quality education for those who are most likely to succeed educationally and economically in the evolving world reality of the post-industrial age.

This orientation toward choice and diversity, especially for those who come to school with a headstart both in terms of cultural and fiscal capital, makes choice a dominant and recurrent theme in conservative policy positions on education. The choice rhetoric of the political right frequently seems to have a strange philosophical kinship with progressivist educational doctrine even though the term 'Conservative' has long been identified in the educational policy world with advocacy of high, *uniform* standards imposed on a curriculum of

core learning shared by *all* students.[7] Despite this educationally progressive hue, however, social policy conservatives are loathe, for
reasons I shall note shortly, to accord expansive choice to minority
persons and especially to persons with low socioeconomic status.

This apparent paradox resolves itself only when one recalls two
basic assumptions of the conservative social policy agenda. First, that
'real' (i.e., academic) education is not, in any case, for the many but
only for the few and, second, that good students come mainly from
families who value education and can be depended upon to search out
quality schools and programs for their children. So long as one views
only a relatively small proportion of the population as capable, in any
case, of turning higher education to the benefit of either self or
society, the idea of high and uniform standards does not conflict with
the educationally progressive goals of diversity and choice. In fact,
what paradoxically emerges from such a set of beliefs is roundabout
endorsement of a sort of equalitarianism for the few and 'choice' for
the many, in which students 'less able to benefit from a strong
academic formation' can choose what they like, provided their aggre-
grate choice is not too costly to the public purse. Students who are
able to benefit, however, and whose parents care to (and can afford
to) ensure that they do, *will use educational choice to equalize upward the
excellence and economic usefulness of the education they receive.* In short, for
the common good of society and for economically efficient investment of scarce educational resources, meaningful freedom to choose,
small-c conservatives argue, is best placed in the hands of those who
will use it to *choose* the best academically-oriented programs. Thus, in
the conservative educational conscience, the most able ultimately
accomplish their own equalization of educational quality and do so
precisely through wise use of educational choice.

The equalitarian social purpose agenda, on the other hand, leads
naturally in the opposite direction, toward more standardization and
control; in fact, toward exactly what has passed for a 'Conservative'
educational policy stance, only in this case a standardization and
control for all, not just for the privileged few. Those who champion
the conservative *educational* agenda, in fact, frequently do so within
the context of remarkably equalitarian assumptions about what society
is and ought to become. Those who most value equalizing opportunity and results argue vigorously that the end result of different curricula for different students is exactly the kind of impermeable social
stratification which radical critics of education since Bourdieu and
Passeron have documented and decried.[8] In short, all forms of differentiated schooling, such educational equalitarians argue, end by

encouraging only 'advantaged' students to meet the standards of the academic and prestigious occupational world. Others are allowed to avoid these standards in the blissful ignorance and meaningless choice of a 'lower' stream or third-rate school. My point here is not to unravel completely the tortured and questionable assumptions under-pinning pure educational conservatism and progressivism, *but to high-light and explain their paradoxical foundations in the larger agendas of social purpose which drive our societies.*

Those who most cherish individual choice (social policy con-servatives) tend naturally to support different schools for different students. Yet, they often become defenders of equalization and stan-dardization, or, more precisely, of efforts to 'raise the educational standards' of traditional losers in the school game even while they zealously defend the right of a certain segment of society to more-or-less exclusive access to schools commonly seen as excellent or out-standing. Rarely, however, is there any question of where the real educational-policy priorities of the small-c conservatives lie. Those who subscribe to a conservative social policy platform *may* endorse either some mandatory, core curriculum and some degree of choice for students they believe to be less able, but they *will* inevitably advance real choice for 'the best and the brightest' as the lynchpin of their educational policy package.

Despite their fundamental value orientation toward equality and standardization in education, those whose first social policy priorities are the equalization of social characteristics and economic opportunity often find themselves espousing, although not without a sense of inconsistency, progressive educational policy with its flexible sense of what knowledge and beliefs schools ought to foster. To act otherwise, they suggest, demeans disadvantaged learners and alienates them from schooling and learning — and schooling should be for all, not just the few. Where social equalitarians do join their conservative opponents in endorsing the principle of educational choice, it is usually with a much more generalistic sense of what that choice might be and for whom. Moreover, as figure 5.1 suggests, equalitarians' prior commit-ment to equality and standardization usually produces a diffuse and subdued vision of and commitment to educational choice. The overall logic of the equalitarian social-policy platform leads much more directly toward a strong, mandated, core curriculum for all students, the less able as well as the more able. Yet, embedded within the equalitarian commitment to equality of educational opportunity, treat-ment and results lies an inevitable link to the choice ethic which is the cornerstone of educational policy derived from social policy conservatism. If education is to be truly universal, which equalitarians insist it must, then it cannot ultimately ignore differences in educational preferences and ability. In short, if schooling is, in any sense, to be for all, differences must ultimately be accommodated, that is, choices must be provided. However uncomfortable the dogmatic equalitarian may be with that idea, one cannot in any very comprehensive sense close down choice if the object is anything close to 'universal' education. The universalism of the the equalitarian's social policy position tends, then, to move toward the otherwise somewhat unnatural goal of enhanced choice, even as the choice and economic efficiency tenets of the conservative social policy platform provide some logical, if rather unnatural support for both choice and strong core curriculum for less-able students.

A striking inversion of principles and terminology, then, can and frequently does occur as larger agendas of social purpose are carried over into the educational arena. The strange bedfellows of the social and educational policy world only occasionally, even at times of social and educational crisis, examine critically the theoretical roots of their competing prescriptions for educational policy. As beliefs about social purpose are pushed to the wall by social change and the economic pressures of the high-technological revolution, the same governments often appear to be moving in two directions at the same time, ostensibly 'beefing up' public school standards even while they seek to strengthen a private educational sector which exists precisely *because* parents and students believe its claim to offer a better education than the public sector can. Short of this overtly dualist policy, jurisdictions such as Minnesota may attempt to offer some sort of 'in-house' voucher system which allows students choice among different *public* schools offering a variety of competing approaches to education housed in a diversified and differentiated, although nominally homogeneous, public system.[9]

The key to unlocking these conceptual and semantic paradoxes is to recall that conservatives, no less than equalitarians, believe that *their* values are right. Thus conservatives would like a certain degree of standardization in the schools, even in all schools, since they, no less than equalitarians, view schooling as a crucially important influence on the values, beliefs and habits of the young. With the easy prosperity of the 1960s, the degree of educational standardization necessary to the survival of a vital free-market seemed relatively small. As good times gave way to hard, and hard times to the harsh reality of the high-tech international marketplace, however, economic productivity and the ability to survive and compete on the world market has become dependent on a steady supply of able and committed technocrats. Increasingly, as the economic hegemony of the traditional giants of the industrialized world is threatened, those committed to the conservative social purpose agenda demand a broad commitment to *their* value set in the schools and are prepared to do whatever needs to be done to ensure some consistency in the beliefs schools foster about economic and social behaviour, as well as about what knowledge is of the most worth and therefore ought to be the most richly rewarded. In short, for small-c conservatives, the pre-eminent conservative principle of free choice is circumscribed in education by a desire to ensure that most young people bring to adulthood a value orientation supportive of the free-market and its consequences. The charge that schools do not provide adequate understanding or appreciation of free-market dynamics and the ethos of private enterprise has become something close to a universal theme in countries that sense their competitive edge growing dull. The conservative doctrine of freedom of choice becomes, in education, the freedom of parents who can afford to do so to choose among schools, but never the freedom of all parents and students to choose any learning they wish.

Within the common school centrepiece scenario, that is

1   mainly public provision for most students,
2   public funding for students in public schools and private funding for those in private schools, and
3   high formal regulation in the public sector but little regulation in the private,

those whose sense of social purpose is dominated by the conservative agenda will value and defend a relatively unfettered existence for private schools. They will, moreover, be offended by the existence of huge publicly operated and funded systems which are pre-eminent examples of government rather than self-provision. They nonetheless support such a system so long as its existence appears economically beneficial and necessary to social harmony and stability. Equalitarians, on the other hand, view such an arrangement with satisfaction because it creates a close-to-universal tax-supported public school system that is at least nominally accessible to all. They would, however, gladly part with unwanted competition from the private sector, competition which they see as unfair and destructive to the common-school ideal.

The common school centrepiece model is rarely, if ever, the arrangement for post-secondary education. Because of the perceived greater private good attached to higher learning, few governments accord a guarantee of universal free access even for the 'well-qualified'. Greater or lesser degrees of private funding and provision are the rule in the post-secondary world, although the evolution of complex and substantial government support programs, both direct and indirect, for universities and technical vocational institutes has necessarily brought in its wake greater government regulation and the evolution of state operated post-secondary institutions of all types. Nonetheless, the rule holds that post-secondary arenas are far too dependent on private money and entrepreneurship to fall into the common-school centrepiece group.

Finally, no attempt to describe educational arrangements would be complete without mention of the huge and growing portion of formal, and especially technical, education provided by industry to its employees. The common school centrepiece arena characteristic of American education and education in the Canadian provinces of British Columbia, Manitoba, New Brunswick and Prince Edward Island coexists frequently with large-scale provision of job-specific education — some at a very high level of technical expertise and theoretical sophistication — by corporate employers. To the extent that schools do less, industry must do more. In the words of an ardent American business advocate of educational reform:

> If current demographic and economic trends continue, American business will have to hire a million new workers a year who can't read, write or count. Teaching them how — and absorbing the lost productivity while they're learning — will cost industry $25 billion a year for as long as it takes. And nobody I know can say how long that will be. Teaching new workers basic skills is doing the schools' product-recall work for them.[10]

The Mixed Private, Public and Public-Alternative School Arena

Many jurisdictions in the Western world have one or more publicly administered and funded alternative school systems. Such arrangements may or may not also allow private schools outside their more comprehensive public education umbrella. Where private schools are allowed they may be more or less tightly regulated by the government. Again, since the mixed private, public and public-alternative school arena arrangement puts most young persons in publicly operated school systems, the question of the commonness of the curriculum is a perennial one, if anything, more vigorously contested because of inevitable program differences arising from special (usually religious) education aims of the competing 'public' school systems. As with single public system arrangements, the range of answers to the common curriculum question varies considerably across its two dimensions of how much of the curriculum should be shared by most students and how long.[11] Answers range, for instance, from complete parallel elementary education systems with no *formal* segregation according to ability in Canadian provinces such as Alberta and Ontario to the early and draconian streaming in the French public and private schools (in France 'private' schools, usually parochial, are generally either 'integrated into public education' or 'associated' by contract with the Ministry of Education).[12] Although recent reforms have abolished streaming in the first cycle of secondary schooling (Grades 6 to 9), French schools continue to separate early those who will go onto a *lycée* and higher education from those who will not. In any case, less than 10 per cent of French students complete secondary education and less than 3 per cent secure a first university degree.[13] French education is a case of public education which embraces or coopts most private education into its mandate,[14] but makes a minimal attempt to enforce one common curriculum on all students.

Many believe the essence of the common school, that is, a schooling experience shared by most pupils in a country or region, can be preserved across fundamental public sector divisions in education. The degree to which public-alternative schools in fact offer such a common experience is very much a matter of the resources (including, not only money and staff, but also student socioeconomic and early childhood education backgrounds) at their disposal, as well as formal curriculum policy. As in the unitary public system model, certain public schools may be arguably more 'exclusive' than the most expensive private schools. Nonetheless, the public systems which such a model generates grow out of the common school ethos of similar schooling experiences for most pupils — an ethos founded on the principle of equal provision, that is educational equalization,[15] an equalitarian ideal which is inevitably missed to a greater or lesser degree in practice. In all arrangements which include large-scale public provision of education, the dominant rationale is social cohesion, sticking people of diverse backgrounds together with a glue of common culture, belief and value commitment that unites them as a nation and makes possible fruitful, peaceful co-existence and economic productivity. How important, valid and useful this rationale is in a world of increasingly multicultural, multilingual and religiously hetero-geneous nations is a matter I will explore in considerable detail in chapter 8.

Religious difference — especially the existence of major popula-tion blocs that differ substantially in religious belief and practice — has long provided the principal *raison d'être* for public provision and fund-ing of alternative school *systems*. More recently, of course, particularly after the ferment and controversy during the 1960s and early 1970s about what schools ought to teach and how, secular alternative schools *within* conventional public boards of education have appeared, but these account for a very small portion of school-age children and adolescents. The major divisions within public education have been religious. The most successful religious group in promoting alterna-tive school systems for the children of its members has unquestion-ably been the Catholic Church.

In Canada, one of the fundamental confederation compromises which made national union possible was Alexander Galt's school compromise, an agreement to entrench in the *British North America Act, 1867* the right to Catholic separate schools for the Catholic minority of Upper Canada (later Ontario) and the right to Protestant separate schools for the English Protestant minority in Lower Canada (later Quebec). As a result of that compromise Ontario and Quebec have come to support, although with quite different governance mod-els, 'public' school systems formed along denominational lines. Parti-cularly in Quebec, where the question of French language survival and dominance is pre-eminent on the social purpose agenda, the old alignment along religious lines is increasingly strained by the arrival of vast numbers of newcomers who are neither Catholic nor Protestant. The Ministry of Education there is consequently seeking some form of accommodation that will conform to the constitution and divide education, at least outside Montreal and Quebec City, along language rather than religious lines. Nonetheless, the fundamental legal impor-tance of the Constitutional guarantee of separate Catholic education continues to be tested and vindicated in Ontario. The recent decision of the Supreme Court of Canada upholding the Ontario government's decision to accord public funding to Catholic high schools and thus 'complete' the Roman Catholic separate school system there to the end of high-school, clearly demonstrates the ongoing legal impor-tance of the Galt compromise.

Elsewhere in Canada, the provinces of Alberta and Saskatchewan provide direct funding for publicly operated Catholic school systems (technically, in Alberta, either the Catholic or public system can be a 'separate' system). An important test case of the terms under which Manitoba joined the confederation, the Manitoba Schools Question, resulted in a federal election and in exemption of Manitoba from any constitutional requirement to provide separate schools for Catholic students. Thus Catholic schools in Manitoba are private and privately funded, although Catholic religious instruction is accommodated in predominantly Catholic population public schools. British Columbia makes available public funds for private schools, of which the majority are Roman Catholic. Only the provinces of Alberta, Ontario, Quebec and Saskatchewan, however, have publicly operated and funded denominational school systems divided along the traditional public/Catholic line.

The same pattern of division into two major 'public' systems, although the legal and governance particulars vary greatly, can be seen in Northern Ireland and Scotland. Although provision is available there for denominations other than the Roman Catholic minority to operate public school systems under the aegis of a Local Education Authority, few such non-Catholic denominational schools now exist.

Other jurisdictions mix more denominations under the umbrella of state provision. Newfoundland in Canada, for instance, recognizes six different types of 'public' school boards, among them Integrated, Roman Catholic, Pentecostal Assemblies and Seventh Day Adventist. Although the provincial Ministry of Education is non-sectarian, it is advised by sectarian Education Councils. England, Wales, Ireland and New Zealand, although with different specific arrangements, fund and provide sectarian education under the public umbrella. In England and Wales such schools include Catholic, Church of England and non-conformist affiliations and are administered as 'voluntary schools' under Local Education Authorities. The situation in England, however, is in considerable flux at the moment, so much so that I believe the United Kingdom must be considered a category of provision, funding and regulation all its own. In Ireland, the 'national schools' which enrol 96 per cent of all pupils, are alternatively Catholic (the vast majority), Presbyterian, Methodist or Church of Ireland (Episcopalian). At the secondary level, however, the Irish arrangement resembles more what I call a pseudo-private school arrangement in that all the 'grammar' schools are private although heavily or completely subsidized.[16]

In every case of dual or multiple public systems examined above, private schools whose students pay fees which account for part or all of the per-pupil expenditures are allowed and generally exist. Varying

---

**The Mixed Private, Public and
Public Alternative School Arena**

Provision: Mainly public. Most students are in one of two or more parallel public
systems but private schools are allowed.
Funding: Public for publicly operated systems and mainly private for private schools,
although some passive support (e.g., tax-exemptions) and even direct-grant support
is occasionally provided.
Regulation: Moderate to high for public schools. Varies for private schools.

For the Conservative Agenda:
  +   More choice and competition because two or more publicly supported
      alternatives exist. Allows private schools to exist, although their freedom is often
      circumscribed where they receive direct government aid.
  −   The educational flagship remains a publicly operated system which, although
      divided, offends principles of minimal government interference and self-provision.
For the Equalitarian Agenda:
  +   Creates close-to-universal publicly supported and operated school systems and
      makes possible fiscal and educational equalization efforts.
  −   Allows private schools to exist, often with minimal government regulation, and
      entrenches some program differences in publicly provided education.

---

degrees and types of public funding are present. These range from property-tax exemptions and free government curriculum materials in multi-system Canadian provinces to major charitable organization income-tax exemptions and incentives such as the exemption from inheritance taxes available to British independent schools who sometimes convince wealthy benefactors to bequeath large sums to them.[17]

In an arena with large, parallel, publicly supported and operated school systems, the regulation of public sector education is never trivial. In addition to all the usual accountability pressures, such an arena has the built-in additional requirement to avoid duplication that the public may perceive as unnecessary or wasteful. As a result, arrangements built around a mix of publicly provided alternatives are unlikely to fall within the purview of options listed on figure 4.5, p. 56. One can therefore assume with some safety a medium or high level of regulation in such education environments.

Figure 4.4, p. 55 suggests what the available options might look like if we assume a generally high degree of regulation in education. Again, a tight regulation of schools that are completely privately operated and funded (option 1) is not likely to be politically acceptable. Legal proscription of all private schools is also unlikely and so, therefore, are options 5, 10 and 15. Finally, full government funding of highly regulated but privately provided education is most unlikely and so option 11 drops from the range of remotely probable arrangements. A 'middle ground' of mixed private and public funding would have features of one of options 7, 8, 9, 12, 13 or 14 *or a similar range of arrangements at a more moderate level of regulation.* In practice, jurisdictions with dual or multiple publicly operated school systems are public system dominant, that is, the vast majority of students attend publicly operated alternative systems. Since this is the case, options 9 and 14 are the most representative of what such systems are like in highly regulated environments. Typically, the mixing of funding occurs along sector lines, that is, the schools of the public systems are wholly funded from some combination of tax fields while the private schools are wholly funded, or almost so, from tuition and donations. Some jurisdictions, of course, such as the Canadian provinces of Alberta and Quebec, make the rare combination of parallel public systems and partial government support for private schools that meet certain statutory requirements.[18] In such cases the link between government funding and at least moderate regulation is evident in the requirements set forth by government for various categories of private schools eligible for government grants.

Where to draw the line between public and private provision is a difficult — increasingly a tortuous — decision. Both the Johnson framework[19] and my own call attention to a range or spectrum of privateness or publicness in education (or any other service) rather than a clear-cut distinction. I examine the complexities which a simple spectrum of publicness masks when I discuss public and pseudo-private environments.[20] For the moment, however, I am considering as public those schools whose governance arrangements are set forth in some detail by law and which are commonly seen by most participants in education and public policy to be operated by an arm or creature of government.

For the Conservative ideologue, the chief attraction of dual or multiple-system public education is that it provides, at least partially, a crude facsimile of free-market attributes, especially inter-system competition. It does so, of course, only to the degree that such systems are truly 'public', that is, open to all. Since such arrangements are typically a response to major religious cleavages in society, universal access to publicly supported alternative systems is usually a contested political question, as it certainly was in the recent struggle over government funding of Catholic secondary schools in Ontario. Perhaps more directly to Conservative tastes, arenas which include more than one publicly operated and funded system usually allow private schools to operate, and occasionally provide some form of direct-grant assistance to them. Where such assistance is provided, some degree of government regulation is always imposed on schools that receive the resulting grants. While the mixed private, public and public-alternative school arrangement retains, from the Conservative view, all of the objectionable properties of near-monolithic state education (e.g., primary reliance on government rather than self-provision, intrusive government regulation and the bureaucratic overhead that comes with it, and so forth), it may introduce some degree of competition within the public sector; but only at the risk of state sponsored duplication of services and facilities.

For equalitarians the mixed private, public and public-alternative school arena offers close-to-universal publicly provided and funded education and thus makes possible a relatively high degree of fiscal equalization and educational standardization. Unfortunately, from the equalitarian perspective, such an arrangement permits private schools to compete with public schools in a relatively free marketplace, provided they do not accept government funding. Perhaps worse, within the equalitarian social purpose agenda with its strong orientation toward homogeneity, such an arrangement inevitably entrenches significant program differences (e.g., religious or instruction or language-use differences) *within publicly provided education.*

The mixed private, public and public-alternative school arena is generically a bit closer to the post-secondary arena in many countries, although the tradition of academic freedom makes imposition of strong government regulation on universities particularly difficult. Nonetheless, many jurisdictions support multiple publicly funded and nominally publicly operated universities and technical institutes. The mechanisms of control, and their effectiveness, vary greatly, but the principle of legislative accountability for public expenditure demands that even public 'multiversities' with their notoriously compendious, amorphous and pliable sense of mission, must provide evidence of responsible use of government grants. The control link tightens to the degree that government research grants form an important share of overall university revenues. Technical institutes have, in the past, often been quite tightly controlled by the sponsoring government, although some countries (notably Japan and England) are currently making vigorous efforts to hive off technical education into the private sector. The fundamental funding, provision and regulation characteristics of the mixed private, public and public-alternative school arena unquestionably resemble existing arrangements for post-secondary education in many, if not most, Western countries today. Public universities and institutes, often with overlapping, and hence competing programs, compete in turn with private universities and institutes which derive less of their total revenues from public funding, although the level of public funding, especially through research grants, available to prestigious, expensive and well-endowed private universities is a subject of sometimes bitter controversy.

The Public and Pseudo-Private Arena

Another orchestration for schooling involves publicly provided education and a heavily subsidized although nominally 'private' education sector. In one sense, this is largely a semantic distinction from the previous category, yet the claim to 'privateness' and common usage of the word must surely be taken into account in assessing the provision of a service. In some countries and regions schools that are heavily funded, and sometimes stringently regulated, by government both claim to be and are perceived to be private. At best, such situations result in a circumscribed freedom of action for such 'private' schools, but the framework I outlined in the previous chapter accommodates such claims. Virtually no area of human enterprise is, in any case, totally exempt from government regulation. The public and pseudo-private arena may allow or proscribe private schools that opt out of government funding and control.

Different countries have evolved public and pseudo-private educational arrangements at various times and for different historical reasons. The two most interesting examples of this type are Holland and Australia. Both illustrate vividly James' point about the importance of religiously motivated entrepreneurialism in promoting alternative systems of publicly funded mass education.[21] Each deals with the regulation of private schools in fundamentally different ways, ways that have profound consequences for the central questions of access to private schooling, the ability of private schools to select their students and the very nature of 'private' schooling in that country.

In Holland, a system of limited and tightly-controlled vouchering of education (and other social services as well) has evolved as a response to major segmentation of Dutch society along cultural and religious lines. The history of Dutch education is, in many respects, an inversion of the history of education in countries which have evolved a common school centrepiece approach to schooling. Holland, in fact, started with a relatively secular, public monopoly at the beginning of the nineteenth century and wound up with a pluralistic 'private' religiously based system by the end. The process culminated in full state funding of private sectarian schools constituted as 'separate but equal' in 1913, an arrangement that was entrenched in the Dutch Constitution in 1917. Ninety-five per cent of primary-level students and 70 per cent of secondary students are now in private schools which enjoy complete government funding of capital expenses and virtually complete funding of operating expenses.[22] In fact, any small group of parents can demand a private government-funded school, although almost all such demands have been by religiously constituted groups. While the ease with which a new school can be established is greater for primary than for secondary schools, it is, by international standards, high for both.

But how private are private schools in the Dutch arrangement? Regulation is extremely high, not surprising in a private sector virtually fully funded by government. From all evidence this is a system within the high regulation domain of figure 4.4, p. 55 and yet heavily dominated by nominally private schools, that is, an option 12 arrangement. What parents may ultimately choose is a school system and a program of religious instruction and little else. For Holland has chosen to limit severely operation of its mainly private educational market by imposing tight limits on the charge-back of fees to parents by *all* private schools. No private school is free to charge much over the basic voucher amount, and most private schools waive even the minimal allowed fee charges for needy students.[23] In addition, teacher numbers, hours and terms of work are set and teacher salaries payed by government for all schools. In James's words:

> Both society, in choosing its system, and private schools, in choosing where they fit into the system, face a trade-off between more autonomy and more [public] funds. In this trade-off, the Dutch private schools have clearly chosen the latter, so long as they can retain their specific denominational or pedagogical identity.[24]

The nature of this choice and the way in which Dutch parents have exercised it, has resulted in young, Dutch people of all socioeconomic classes being quite proportionally represented among the various 'private' school types. The only exception appears to be that migrant workers are disproportionately represented in the public or municipally operated schools.[25] Since selection by price rationing is severely limited and all schools practice early and extreme streaming by 'ability', Dutch school *systems* have not stratified by socioeconomic status. On the other hand, the flow to different tracks or streams within the various competing systems and schools is highly correlated with socioeconomic status and so the Dutch formula is not an answer to the equalitarian dream.[26]

The cooption of private schools by the government in Australia is less extreme — or perhaps just less advanced. A history of growing Commonwealth support for private schools in Australia has been punctuated by bitter battles over the classic private-school support questions of access, equity and elitism. What finally forced government action — and mainly at the federal level although education is a state responsibility in Australia — was emergence, in 1969, of a network of Roman Catholic private schools perceived by advocates and opponents alike as appalling in their lack of facilities and qualified staff. The immigration of the 1960s left Australia with a large and growing Catholic population that demanded, and eventually won, government funding for Catholic private schools. Interestingly, the Australian constitution contains a clause prohibiting excessive entanglement of church and state that is virtually identical to the First Amendment of the American constitution. The Australian courts, however, unlike the American supreme court, have consistently upheld a very loose interpretation of their establishment clause, an interpretation which has easily allowed government funding of religious schools.

In Australia, the Fraser Government (1975–83) actually preceded the Thatcher Government in England in embarking on educational policy aimed at encouraging voluntary effort, enhancing parental choice and protecting and promoting the 'excellence' which it ascribed to certain expensive private schools in the various Australian states.[27] The Fraser Government found in the Catholic education crisis of the late 1960s and early 1970s an opportunity to show government support for education more broadly defined than just state schooling.[28] Although the state governments, which have primary constitutional responsibility for education in Australia, were still spending only 5.4 per cent of their educational budget on non-government schools in 1981–2, the Commonwealth Government was sending 46.7 per cent of its billion-dollar education budget to private schools.[29] The importance of recent public contribution to 'private' schools in Australia is most clearly shown by the fact that, in 1980, 80 per cent of non-government schools were getting 80 per cent of costs from public funds.[30]

Yet, not all private schools are primarily supported out of public funds in Australia. Indeed, much of the controversy about public funding has revolved around a relatively small number of private schools that charge relatively large fees and yet continue to receive substantial government grants.[31] This inclusion in private school funding measures of schools that charged very large per-pupil fees occurred against a backdrop of funding constraint in public schools, especially in primary education.[32] A major plank in the election platform of the Hawke Labour Government in 1983 was a phase-out of private school funding — especially private funding to schools on a party 'hit list' of elite, well-endowed (as well as non-Catholic) private schools.[33] In the event, all private school constituencies, including Catholic school supporters, rallied to the support of government funding for private schools in the name of enhanced access and choice for all. The government was forced to content itself with pegging Commonwealth funding for the wealthier schools at existing levels until 1992.[34]

That Australian private schools are subject to considerable regulation, however, is evident from the relatively massive reporting responsibilities laid upon them by the Commonwealth and state governments.[35] Accountability is obviously an important part of the agenda of public funding for private education in Australia. While a good deal of control is left to schools (and to the Catholic school systems) themselves, Australian private schools are not 'independent' in the same sense as British independent schools. Whether this is due to the instruments of aid for private education (i.e., direct grants to schools in Australia, for instance, versus 'assisted places' scholarships in England) is debatable. Claims and counterclaims are rampant in the literature on public funding of private schools about the possibility of meaningfully distinguishing between funds 'directed to parents' and 'funds directed to schools'.[36] In any case, Australian private schools have substantial reporting duties to their sponsor governments and are, therefore, in some sense, pseudo-private — or at least less than independent if independence means freedom from direct government control.

In a public and pseudo-private arena, provision of educational services, is, at least nominally, split between the two sectors. Funding, however, is often predominantly, or at least significantly, from public sources. Not surprisingly, government regulation of private schools in such an arena, tends to be high where the proportion of public source revenues for such schools is high. The most highly regulated current case is probably the Dutch, where virtually every detail of finance and program, including the all-important question of freedom to charge fees, is centrally controlled.

What such an arrangement offers the Conservative ideologue is

---

The Public and Pseudo-Private Arena

Provision: Mixed private and pseudo-public. Proportion of enrolments in private schools high and many programs in public schools privately provided.

Funding: Private and public for both types of provision. More public funds to private schools and more private funds to public schools. Strong restraint on public funds to public schools.

Regulation: Initially extremely high for public-sector schools, eventually much lower. Low to non-existent for private schools (except for assisted places eligibility approval).

For the Conservative Agenda:
  + A much freer educational market with more choice for more parents and children.
  − Self-provision compromised by continued public funding and maintenance of a pseudo-public system for pupils not in private schools.

For the Equalitarian Agenda:
  + Some degree of government provision and manipulation of resource equity in education preserved.
  − Everything else. Privatization has largely overridden the principles of standardization and educational equity.

---

more choice for more parents and students than either of the previous arrangements for schools, *provided private schools do not become mere satellites or constituents of a highly uniform public provision.* In reality this tends to mean that, to be distinctive, private schools must continue to derive some significant portion of their revenues from non-government sources. Therefore, the more such an arrangement for schooling fosters the pseudo-private reality of full government funding with nominally independent governance, the less acceptable it is within a conservative sense of social purpose oriented toward meaningful choice (especially for the 'most able').

Conversely, combining public provision with a pseudo-private, publicly funded sector means that some (in the Dutch case, *all*) private schools can be regulated more or less closely by the government. Moreover, pseudo-private schools can be included in various schemes of educational and fiscal equalization. All this is to the delight of equalitarians. Unfortunately, however, the price for such delights is allowing private schools to exist (however unprivate their corporate life may be) *and to foster significant and socially important differences in beliefs, values and culture and, moreover, to do so at public expense.* Worse still, from the equalitarian viewpoint, unless private school fees are severely limited as in the Dutch case, such an arrangement does nothing about expensive elitist private schools which price ration their educational and social benefits. Indeed, as the perennial but futile efforts of the Labour Party in Australia to end government grants to such schools demonstrates, arrangements of this type may do little more than marginally lower tuition fees in the best private schools, reductions that fail to extend substantially the socioeconomic-status spectrum of students who can attend such schools but nonetheless provide an appearance of unbiased support for 'all forms' of schooling.

In one way or another, governments which rely to a considerable degree on pseudo-private arrangements for schooling seek to follow the 'medium system' path which Chalmers enunciated on behalf of a Scottish Church that had helped create, without compulsion, a 'habit of general education' in the Highlands of the early nineteenth century. A 'medium system', one which combines substantial public 'endowment' with private fees, seemed to Chalmers the best compromise between stifling initiative on the one hand, and excluding the poor on the other.[37] Such a sense of educational purpose clearly derives from a middle-ground of social purpose, one which compromises and blends the principles of the conservative and equalitarian social purpose agendas. It steadfastly refuses to commit to a public monolith and champions the value of direct, individual investment in schooling — in a word some degree of self-provision. Students who know that their parents pay 'directly' for their education are likely to be, the 'middle-ground' argument goes, more diligent and hence successful. Yet, what is to be expressly avoided, and can only be avoided with public funding, is the educational disenfranchisement, especially the denial of even formal access to schools, of whole social classes.

Conclusion

Three major orchestrations of schooling occur, albeit with important thematic variations, in most developed and undeveloped countries in the Western world. Where those who shape educational policy are most imbued with a social purpose agenda focussed on equalization, standardization and extensive government involvement in education, some variation of the common school centrepiece arena is the most likely result. Large, nominally homogeneous state school systems will enrol the majority of students. Privately operated and funded schools with considerable autonomy provide educational services for the rest.

If, however, a society is divided into major cultural and/or religious groups, one of two basic models usually develops. In the first, private, public and public-alternative schools proffer their services to the tastes and preferences of those who choose, and can gain access to, each type of school. In the second, a pseudo-private sector is added which caters principally to cultural and religious groups that wish a high level of public funding and freedom to shape a distinctive cultural and/or religious environment for schooling. The price such groups inevitably pay, of course, is government regulation proportional to government funding.

The connection between agendas of social and educational purpose is by no means simple or linear but it is, nonetheless, important. Those committed to free-market *laissez-faire* capitalism with generally favour policies which permit and encourage private initiative and entrepreneurship in education. They will, however, also favour sufficient standardization and control over the schooling experienced by most young people to enable a relatively free national and world market to exist and function, that is, they will want some public mandate to inculcate in all young persons beliefs and values friendly to *their* principles. Those committed to equalitarian principles, on the other hand, will devise models emphasizing central control, universality, equalization, standardization and government rather than self-provision.

The current efforts of the Tory Government in Britain to reform schooling arrangements in the United Kingdom seem to be moving in new and unusual directions at the same time that they retrace some very familiar ground. In any case, they present a distinctive face for schooling arrangements, distinctive enough, to warrant a chapter of their own.

Notes

1 See pp. 8 and 15.
2 See Figure 4.1, p. 50.
3 See, for instance, James, E. 'The public/private division of responsibility for education: An international comparison', *Economics of Education Review*, 6 (1987), p. 11.
4 For an up-to-date estimate of the proportion of students in public and private schools in the US, see Bruce Cooper, Donald McLaughlin and Bruno Manno. 'The latest word on private school growth', *Teachers College Record*, 85 (Fall 1983), p. 97.
5 John Bergen, 'The Private School Movement in Canada', *Education Canada*, 21 (June 1981), p. 8.
6 George Thomas Kurain, *Major Countries: Algeria-Hungary*, vol. I of *World Education Encyclopedia* (New York: Facts on File Publications, 1988), pp. 452–4.
7 For a detailed exploration of the paradox of Conservative social ethos combined with centralized educational planning, see the discussion of

current educational policy developments in Great Britain in Chapter 6 of
this volume.

8 For the origins of the whole vocabulary of radical critique of schooling
based on a conception of schooling as classicist symbolic violence, see
Pierre Bourdieu and Jean-Claude Passeron, *Reproduction in Education,
Society and Culture*, trans. Richard Nice (London: Sage Publications), pp.
3–68.

9 Nancy J. Perry, 'Saving the schools: How business can help', *Fortune*,
118 (November 1988), pp. 42–56.

10 David T. Kearns 'An education recovery plan for America', *Phi Delta
Kappan*, 69 (April 1988), p. 566.

11 See p. 67.

12 Kurain, *Major Countries: Algeria-Hungary*, vol. I of *World Education
Encyclopedia, op cit ,* p. 410.

13 *Ibid.*

14 This is so depite controversial efforts of the French government in the
early 1980s to distance itself from parochial education.

15 See p. 15.

16 For much of the information in the preceding five paragraphs, I am
indebted to an unpublished report on sectarian schooling arrangements
prepared by Stephen Lawton in 1985. (See p. 82 and following.)

17 Geoffrey Walford, 'How dependent is the independent sector?' *Oxford
Review of Education*, 13 (October 1987), p. 287.

18 Recent changes in the the Alberta *School Act* suggest a dramatic move
toward strengthening the private sector in Alberta education with both
government money and moral support. In fact, Alberta could be moving
toward a much more even sharing of overall enrolment by private and
public schools, in spirit, at least toward what I discuss as the Public and
Pseudo-Private model (p. 82). See Margaret Durnin, 'The new Alberta
school act', *Our Schools, Our Selves*, 1 (October 1988), pp. 96–105.

19 See p. 49.

20 See p. 82.

21 Estelle James, 'The public/private division of responsibility for education: An international comparison,' *Economics of Education Review*, 6
(February 1987), p. 1; and 'Benefits and costs of privatized public services: Lessons from the Dutch educational system', *Comparative Education*, 28 (November 1984), p. 605.

22 James, 'Benefits and costs of privatized public services: Lessons from the
Dutch educational system', *op cit.*, pp. 608–9.

23 Given the high relative level of the per-pupil voucher available, the
marginal cost of providing for an additional student is almost always less
than the value of the voucher, so accepting needy students makes economic sense for private schools in the Dutch milieu. Given the fact that
Dutch tax-payers pay a premium in cost efficiency (James estimates this
as high as 10–20 per cent) for their differentiated pseudo-private system,

there is almost certainly considerably excess capacity in most schools private and public.

24 *Ibid.*, p. 613.

25 *Ibid.*, p. 620.

26 *Ibid.*, p. 621.

27 Tony Edwards, John Fitz, and Geoff Whitty, 'Private schools and public funding: A comparison of recent policies in England and Australia', *Comparative education*, 21 (March 1985), p. 30.

28 D. Doyle, 'A din of inequity: Private schools reconsidered', *Teachers College Record*, 82 (May 1981), p. 671.

29 Michael Hogan, *Public vs. Private Schools: Funding and Directions in Australia* (Victoria: Penguin Books Australia Ltd.), p. 83.

30 Edwards T., Fitz J. and Whitty G., 'Private schools and public funding: A comparison of recent policies in England and Australia', *op cit.*, p. 32.

31 Anglican secondary schools, for instance, were, on average, deriving 60.2 per cent of their total revenues ($1437 per student) from fees in 1979. Catholic high schools, on the other hand, derived only 17.9 per cent ($208 per pupil) from fees and 58 per cent from government sources. See Michael Hogan, *Public vs. Private Schools: Funding and Directions in Australia* (Victoria: Penguin Books Australia Ltd.), p. 103.

32 Hogan, *Public vs. Private Schools*, *op cit.*, p. 86.

33 *Ibid.*, p. 1.

34 Edwards T., Fitz J. and Whitty G., 'Private schools and public funding: A comparison of recent policies in England and Australia', *op cit.*, p. 30.

35 Hogan, *Public vs. Private Schools*, *op cit.*, p. 116.

36 See, for instance, Edwards, Fitz and Whitty, 'Private schools and public funding: A comparison of recent policies in England and Australia', *op cit.*, p. 37.

37 R.D. Anderson, 'Education and the state in nineteenth-century Scotland', *The Economic History Review*, 2nd. Series, 36 (November 1983), p. 521.

Chapter 6

The English Experiment:
Privatize and Standardize

> In the past few years, however, a loss of confidence in public
> enterprises in general, and in state education in particular, has
> led people ... to question the assumption that education is
> best conceived as a compulsory and universal service both
> financed and provided by governments. Overt displays of lack
> of confidence may be no more than pragmatic adjustments to
> declining public belief in the wealth-creating and opportunity-
> creating effects of schooling. Often, however, they have been
> expressions of political preference for greater consumer choice
> or for a transfer of more of the cost of services to their users,
> or an assertion of belief in the particular capacity of the private
> sector to maintain academic standards and social values judged
> to be in danger outside it.[1]

> ... the major problem with public education is that the rich
> can exit. If the rich had to remain, they would exercise their
> power to bring about reforms.[2]

These two divergent perceptions capture much of the thrust and
parry of current debate about educational purpose, and its relationship
to the larger issues of social purpose. On the one hand, recent
and persistent electoral success in a number of OECD countries by those
who endorse the conservative social purpose agenda clearly reflects
considerable disenchantment with public institutions generally, public
schools perhaps foremost among them. On the other, the primary line
of counter-attack from champions of equalization and standardization
is that what is wrong with large systems of public provision is mainly
the power of the rich to opt out, a belief that if all were compelled

to participate in them, all would be concerned about the quality of public institutions and, consequently, that quality would necessarily improve. One argument leads to government disengagement and privatization; the other leads toward state sponsored universalism and compulsion. Great Britain is currently experimenting with an educational policy collage which appears, at first glance, to stand astride both horns of this dilemma, trying simultaneously to privatize the schools on a relatively large scale and in diverse ways, yet to impose strong and pervasive central control and standards on maintained (publicly administered and supported) schools. Why the Tory government, and especially the current administration, has organized this crusade aimed in two apparently opposite directions is the subject of much speculation — and of the final section of this chapter. How and why the Tory Government is attempting to orchestrate this cacophonous amalgam of two radically different themes is the main subject of this chapter.

The British government appears to be writing, or attempting to write, a new arrangement for schooling that is qualitatively different from any of the major types considered in the previous chapter. Nor can education be considered to be a lesser star in the current British public policy arena. With the Falklands conflict disposed of, education was a major issue of the 1987 campaign, an issue which Thatcher's Tories used to sell another Tory majority to the British electorate. The bywords of that campaign were educational 'choice' on the one hand, and 'standards' on the other.[3] The economic survival of England depended, the Tories assured the British electorate, on higher quality education in the United Kingdom and the only way to that higher quality was to travel at one time the seemingly divergent paths of more choice on the one hand, and higher and more universal standards on the other.

General Background: Immediate History and Status Quo

As it has operated in recent years, the English schooling arrangement most closely approximates what I have called the mixed private, public and public-alternative school arena.[4] In simplest terms, that arena includes a private sector combining the prestigious English 'public' schools (although they have rechristened themselves 'independent' to escape the political stigma of the elite image associated with 'public' schools in England) with a considerable variety of newer

The English Experiment: Privatize and Standardize

independent schools while the government itself maintains a mix of non-sectarian and sectarian schools. In general, private schools have accounted in the recent past for about 5 per cent of all elementary and secondary enrolments with about one-quarter of these in the elite 'public', mainly boarding, schools solidly rooted in the British public school tradition. The precise details of public-sector arrangements are slightly different in Scotland from those in England and Wales as a result of a considerably different historical context and evolution. Nonetheless, Scottish public-sector education is organized within the same Local Education Authority (LEA) arrangement that prevails in England and Wales except that there are no school-level boards of governors in Scotland with the result that the Education Committees of Scottish LEAs have somewhat tighter control than their English counterparts. As well, Roman Catholic schools in Scotland are not 'voluntary' in the same sense as they are in England and Wales, that is, Scottish Roman Catholic schools are financed and operated by the LEAs although certain powers are reserved to the Catholic church.[5] What is important, however, is that fundamentally the Scottish arrangement, like the British to date, is an example of a mixed private, public and public-alternative arrangement in the sense discussed in the last chapter.[6]

Two categories of publicly supported schools exist in the Britain. In England and Wales all schools of both types have been, until recently, operated under the auspices of an LEA with responsibility for educational governance falling to the Education Committee of the responsible LEA. The composition of such committees varies, but would often include thirty to forty members, three-quarters of whom are aldermen or councillors. The other quarter typically combines representatives of religious groups (principally Church of England, Roman Catholic and non-conformist), teachers, parents, business, labour and institutions of higher learning. Each committee appoints a chief education officer.[7] The largest LEA, that for London, has recently been abolished.

The major governance distinction among publicly maintained schools created by *The Education Act, 1944* is that between county schools and the voluntary schools. County or 'council' schools, are those established and maintained directly by an LEA while voluntary schools are established and maintained by some other agency, usually a religious organization, under one of three possible sets of terms for control and funding. Voluntary schools can be controlled, aided or run under the terms of a special agreement. Controlled schools are fully LEA funded for both operating and capital costs. In return, controlled schools must accept LEA appointment of two-thirds of their governing boards. Aided schools, on the other hand, receive full funding for operating expenses but must raise 20 per cent of capital costs on their own, usually from a sponsoring religious group. Aided schools appoint two-thirds of the members of their boards of governors and therefore obtain a very high level of local control over staffing and curriculum, a control limited in the past mainly by state teacher certification and a system of periodic subject exams. Such exams, however, were *not* national exams in the sense that all students received the same exam content.[8] Aided schools have tended to be academic rather than comprehensive and often have facilities superior to county schools in their LEA area because of the additional donations they attract from sponsoring religious communities. In certain cases special agreements govern the relations between LEAs and voluntary schools.

Each major religious group has had a commission overseeing their schools. The jurisdiction of these religious groups, however, has not included élite public schools of the same denomination and thus their direct influence has been confined to the voluntary schools. The armslength relationship between English voluntary schools (especially 'aided' schools) and their LEAs evolved out of a relationship between the Catholic minority and other Britons much more tentative and uncertain than that between Scotch Catholics and the overwhelming majority of Scots who were Presbyterian and felt completely unthreatened by the Catholic minority in their midst.[9] In any case, the aided school category has provided a sort of separate religiously-based genre of publicly supported and delivered education operating under LEA auspices.

Until the mid-1970s a small group of independent ('private') secondary schools, typically academic or 'grammar' schools, received direct grants from the Department of Education and Science to offset the fees for a quarter of their students. Termination of this direct-grant program led a number of private Roman Catholic schools to opt into voluntary, 'aided' status. It also led to demands from existing independent schools for a new form of aid to broaden access to such schools. The transition to a new scheme of assistance for independent schools in Britain is the first part of the story of how the Tory Government appears to be working toward a qualitatively different kind of schooling arrangement in the United Kingdom. Driven by strong ideological commitment to the principles of the Conservative social agenda,[10] and by public perception that England was sinking in the international marketplace largely because the schools were failing to produce economically productive workers and thinkers, the Tories have embarked on policies which could rewrite both the social contract and the educational purpose agenda in England — or perhaps merely reinstate older ones that were formally abandoned some time ago.

Toward a Private and Pseudo-Public Arena?

Educational reform in England during the latter years of the Thatcher administration meant two major, and seemingly contradictory, policy thrusts. On the one hand, Thatcher's ministers were increasingly encouraging educational privatization in all its guises, while on the other they were imposing a strong centralization of government control over publicly delivered education and its various curricula. One of the primal assumptions of the Conservative social purpose agenda is that 'quality requires choice, and choice requires private enterprise'.[11] If one accepts this dictum as the primary concern underlying public policy-making in education, the dominant goal of such policy-making becomes relatively simple: how can one best orchestrate the maximum politically acceptable degree of private control and private funding; in a word, to what extent and by what means can government encourage both self-provision and retreat from universal government provision. In a real-world public policy arena, how can government fulfil the 'moral purpose' of privatization, 'to shift the responsibility for learning from the state (or teachers employed by the local authority) to parents'.[12]

Privatizing Schooling in England: A Campaign on Many Fronts

It would be wrong to suggest that privatization has largely replaced public provision, funding and control of education in England. It would be equally wrong, however, to suggest that the British government has not made considerable, concerted and diverse efforts to bolster the private sector in education in the United Kingdom since accession of the first Thatcher government. These efforts, moreover, have occurred against a backdrop of extreme spending restraints in the 'maintained' (LEA sponsored schools) thus inviting the charge from teacher organizations and Labour Party alike that the government is indeed set on a course of replacing public-sector schools with private in Britain.

How has the government sought to enhance the role of private enterprise in British education? The answer is complex and multi-faceted, and may ultimately involve, to an important degree, the current draconian attempts of the responsible ministers to rein in the curriculum of the maintained schools and recast it in a very traditional mold. At the least, the Tory privatization campaign involves the following major lines of attack:

1 strong ideological support for the independent schools includ-ing overt support from government members for the proposi-tion that independent schools frequently offer, in fact are inherently capable of, a quality of education impossible in the maintained schools;[13]
2 encouraging maintained schools to purchase more of the ser-vices (e.g., inservice training) and materials they use on the open market rather than internally through their LEA;
3 encouraging the development of school-level governance bodies responsive to the wishes and preferences of parents;
4 encouraging, even necessitating, the purchase at *private ex-pense* of educational materials and services in the maintained schools;[14]
5 encouraging and enabling the purchase at *public expense* of educational services in private institutions;[15] and
6 most recently, encouraging LEA sponsored schools to opt out of the public sector.

In practice, such principles have translated into a wide variety of administrative action which has served both to strengthen privately delivered education and to blur the distinction between private and public delivery of education. As Pring points out, this blurring is by no means unintentional.[16] Among the more notable trends in this regard are privatization of in-service; a new role for schools and uni-versities as accountable 'cost centres'; encouragement of 'covenanting' (solicitation of voluntary contributions) as a form of private support for the maintained schools; severe restrictions on both operating and capital budgets for the maintained schools, and solicitation and accept-ance of commercial sponsorship, for schools, educational materials and even teaching positions.

With regard to privatization, the policy handwriting is clearly on the wall in the sense that the government has acted on and continues to act on its intent to make the public schools more responsive to market forces and to their local communities, but decidedly not to local education authorities. No longer is in-service to be determined mainly by LEA administration and considered to be a fiefdom of the universities. No longer should schools, or universities for that matter, have any *a priori* right to either students or service contracts. The idea is to promote freer competition for all kinds of educational patronage, including the most basic one of attendance. Even in maintained schools, the trend is toward funding levels which 'maintain' them in ever more straitened circumstances, and parents and benefactors are frequently approached (rather than pressured, of course) to 'covenant' with their school to help support programs which complement and enrich the minimal state-supported program.[17] By its budgetary parsimony the government has, in effect, encouraged the maintained schools to turn to private-sector largesse for educational materials and more. If schools lack the money to buy resource materials, they can at least accept them from 'public spirited' organizations who make them available to them without charge, or at attractively subsidized prices. In fact, if the schools lack funds to provide programs, classrooms and even teachers, the private sector is sometimes quite inclined to help provide them. This is especially true in areas where a particular company has a heavy investment and wishes to attract well-qualified parents sensitive to the quality and breadth of educational opportunities open to their children. It is much less true, of course, in less economically favoured areas.

That such private-sector largesse is often not without an agenda of its own has not, of course, escaped the attention of critics of this particular brand of privatization. Starving the maintained schools, while it may draw private resourcing into publicly administered schools and thus reduce the spending pressure of public education in general on the public budget, also invites corporate contributors to produce learning materials which cast their particular interests in the most favourable light, and to sponsor programs — and even teachers — that foster beliefs and values of direct or indirect benefit to them. Such corporate benefactors are more likely, in short, to steer educational materials and programs toward support of their particular interests than toward social cohesion and the common good. Private support inevitably exacts a price in private control of the curriculum and value agenda of public education.[18] Moreover, this particular form of privatization, that is, blurring the boundaries between private and public in schools operated publicly (at least nominally) can make few claims to address comprehensively any of the equity dimensions of education. Communities endowed with generous corporate benefactors and many 'covenantable' families, presumably high-income families with school-age children, are likely to have rich and diverse educational programs in their public-sector schools, while communities with neither will assuredly get only whatever minimum program is publicly funded. As Pring warns, in many areas in England that minimum increasingly excludes music and art, as well as physical and remedial education, so that access to such programs requires the good fortune of being in a school with private and corporate sponsorship — if not of being in an altogether private school.[19]

A second price of privatizing by encouraging direct private resource contribution to publicly operated schools is surrender of some of whatever ability government may have to adjust resource inputs on the basis of perceived differences in need and cost.[20] At a more general level, transferring a significant portion of the cost of publicly provided education to private sources offers a means for denying the demand of the masses for better education. In England, with its extremely poor economic track record in the late 1970s and early 1980s, perhaps even more so than in many other countries, the economic rationale for education is under close scrutiny. If we are all becoming citizens of a world in which the demand for large numbers of moderately and highly educated persons is rapidly diminishing, 'self-provision' can serve as a political euphemism to justify saying no to the 'excess' educational demands and aspirations of the masses — educational demands and aspirations which have increasingly limited public and private economic returns on investment in them — particularly when compared to investment in the education of a technocratic and managerial élite and in leading-edge production technology.

Thatcher's Tories, however, have extended the ambit of their privatization efforts well beyond attempts to funnel more private and less public funds into the maintained schools. A second major initiative has extended direct public funding for privately operated (independent) schools. In addition to the not uncommon advantages of publicly funded and provided initial teacher education and of charitable status for income tax purposes, British independent schools have long enjoyed the particular advantage of offering a complete exemption from inheritance tax. Schools could claim *all* of the bequest of any number of benefactors. Taken as a whole, the package of tax benefits available to British independent schools have helped them significantly and compare very favourably to tax benefits available in other jurisdictions.[21] Whether or not such benefits are 'tax expenditures' and hence constitute 'government aid' to private schools, of course, depends on one's view of the thorny problem of tax expenditures in general — and ultimately, some believe, on whether the government has an *a priori* claim on *all* income and merely concedes some to private wage earners and private and corporate entrepreneurs.[22] What seems certain is that the British government would be up to £178 million per year richer and private schools the same amount poorer if all tax concessions and similar benefits for private schools were to end.[23] On the other hand, there is no question, in Britain or elsewhere, that the cost of accommodating private school students in publicly operated schools would be far greater than the value of all indirect benefits accorded to them. In short, governments experience a net saving on educational expenditures because of the existence of private schools, a saving which almost always far outweighs any tax income which they forgo in favour of such schools.

Until the Labour government, which preceded the first Thatcher administration, ended the 'Direct Grant Scheme', private schools had, at least theoretically, a means of obtaining some direct subsidies from the government. The Labour government ended the arrangement in pursuit of its commitment to public comprehensive education, a commitment which saw private, and especially the traditional British 'public' schools as anathema to a universalistic, equalitarian public system for all. The private, now independent, schools themselves, however, had been less than pleased with the Direct Grant Scheme. The principal problem with the scheme, from their point of view, however, was that it was honoured more in the breach than in the observance. Because LEA cooperation was required — LEAs had to 'send' students — and because the independent schools were inevitably in competition with LEA-sponsored schools, the Direct Grant Scheme had been almost inoperative, a recipe for stalemate. For the most part, LEAs didn't send students and independent schools didn't get grants.[24]

With the accession to power of the Thatcher government in 1979 and its Conservative social purpose agenda, the independent schools recognized fertile political ground and began sowing the seeds of a new grant program. A wisely constructed grant plan for private schools, its advocates claimed, would extend the range of choice available to parents and make the excellence of the independent schools accessible to all — or at least to more. The plan finally agreed upon by the government was the Assisted Places Scheme (ASP). In the parlance of the Department of Education and Science (DES), the scheme was designed to 'give able children a wider range of educational opportunity'.[25]

The initial enthusiasm of the Thatcher government was somewhat tempered by the furore which erupted over the magnitude of the initial ASP budget proposal, and the relatively small number of targeted beneficiaries. At a time when the roof was falling in on the maintained schools — often literally as well as fiscally — the government proposed to divide £55 million each year in England and Wales among 12,000 'needy' students.[26] Both opposition and teachers cried foul — far too much to far too few at a time when the maintained schools were bleeding. In response, the government scaled down the APS budget to £34 million and divided it much more sparingly among 21,400 pupils whose financial need would be assessed by a means test applied to their parents. Sixty per cent of APS recipients were supposed to have come from maintained schools but this target was achieved only in the case of the 11+ cohort in 1986/7.[27] In fact, qualifying students have tended to be offspring of single-parent families with other children already in private schools. Few working-class children receive APS places. To obtain a place under the scheme, a student must first be selected by a school approved to offer places under it and then pass a means test. Not surprisingly, those who meet both criteria are typically middle-class children whose families have fallen on hard times.[28]

The Assisted Places Scheme was sold politically as an aid to able but needy students, not as direct government aid to schools. ASP was conceived as a limited voucher scheme that would allow underprivileged but gifted students a chance to go to the best schools without forging a direct link of government support to independent schools. As foreseen, however, by those who contend that no valid distinction can be made between support for students and support for schools,[29] British independent schools rose to the APS challenge with a haste and dexterity that Labour and the public-sector education establishment found altogether unseemly, if not suspicious. Many participating schools are running up to 50 per cent of their enrolment places under the APS programme. APS is very likely 'allowing independent schools to remain open by filling places at the public expense'. Worse still, from the point of view of public-sector spokespersons and equalitarian principles, APS allows independent schools to cream off the academically most promising students who would otherwise, perforce, have to attend maintained schools.[30] The result is a government sponsored brain-drain from publicly operated schools in Britain, further evidence, critics claim, of the government's contempt for and long-term commitment to undoing universal, comprehensive education and its equalitarian social purpose charter.

Yet the surest indicator of the government's charted course may be its emerging City Technology Colleges (CTC) scheme. The government is moving quite dramatically to privatize vocational education — and thereby provide some demand driven basis for the education of relatively high ability but non-academically oriented 11–19-year-olds.[31] To be sure, England has not greatly distinguished itself from other major European countries in the degree to which most students remain in school. In a move very reminiscent of the current evolving private governance arrangement for technically oriented junior colleges in Japan (over 80 per cent of which are private),[32] the government has decided that technical and vocational education should increasingly be the purview of private institutions that will rise or fall on the marketability of the skills they purvey to their students. An important difference, of course, is that the Japanese build on a national passion for education (95 per cent of Japanese students finish upper secondary schools, a three-year period during which all students must pay fees)[33] while England begins with a strong tradition of high dropout rates and considerable indifference among a substantial portion of the population to higher learning in any form. Moreover, to date, the private sector has hardly been in a rush to contribute to the development of the City Technology College scheme in any major way.[34]

Nonetheless, many read the City Technology Colleges scheme as a Tory paradigm for the ultimate and complete privatization, and perhaps voucherization, of schooling in Great Britain.[35] Nor has the university sector escaped the Tory passion to make education 'responsive to the marketplace'. The most egregious example is clearly the 'private' University of Buckingham (with the former Prime Minister, Mrs Thatcher, herself as patron) but other very significant changes are occurring within the older 'public' universities as well. First, such universities are experiencing the same erosion of government financial support their primary- and secondary-level counterparts lived with throughout the Thatcher years. Second, the British government appears to be working hard to abolish both the principle and the fact of tenure for university faculty.[36] How better, they argue, to unfreeze an ossified tertiary education system than to restore competition? How better to restore competition than to rid universities of faculty who no longer produce because their survival is no longer contingent on producing? While such a logic completely overlooks the reasons why the tenure system evolved in the first place, namely the *competition* among universities to attract and retain first-class scholars and teachers, it does appeal to the free-market, produce-or-perish ethos. If universities — or primary schools — are 'cost-centres', they ought always and everywhere to justify their costs by criteria of market selection. Finding such a conceptualization to be at odds with the very idea of education in any liberal sense, and with the idea of university in particular, does nothing to reduce its appeal to those strongly committed to the Conservative social purpose agenda — especially when they have taken the helm of a battered and beleaguered national economy.

What is indisputable is that the government, especially former Secretary of State for Education, Kenneth Baker, has initiated educational policies which lead to a qualitatively different mix of schooling provisions; one in which private schools are free to solicit the patronage of academically talented but impecunious students and then to admit them at government expense, or with heavy government fee subsidies. The emerging mix in Great Britain is becoming less and less a public/private mix and more a mix of private (although in some cases heavily dependent on public funding through the APS program) and pseudo-public schools. Although relatively few maintained schools are expected to accept recent government encouragement to opt out of the public sector and establish themselves as private schools (despite the fact that Mrs Thatcher publicly 'look[ed] forward to a situation where "most schools" would choose to opt out of the state system'),[37] 'controlled' and 'voluntary' schools are being pressed hard to find more of their operating and even capital resources in the private sector.

To the extent that the maintained schools become directly dependent on private and corporate largesse for survival and operation, they become less public and more pseudo-public, that is, they wear the official public mantle but are, in part at least, creatures of the benefactors who grant them the means to carry out their schooling mandate. For those convinced of the inherent evils of big government and large-scale public provision of social services, this is far from an undesirable outcome. Indeed, it is all the more useful if it proves a stepping stone toward the more complete privatization prefigured by the preferred Thatcher–Baker approach to the Technology Colleges.[38]

What is missed, of course, in the rationale for such an arrangement are the issues of equity and standardization upon which the equalitarian social purpose agenda is founded and toward which equalitarian educational policy most naturally flows.[39] Yet no government, however Conservative, can afford to overlook these issues entirely. On the heels of the 1987 election and under the direction of Kenneth Baker, the Thatcher educational reform program has recently acquired a new face, one which appears to speak to these issues in a politically highly marketable way. At first glance, however, it is a face which seems as unlike the privatization face as the tragic and comic masks of classical Greek theatre are unlike one another.

The National Curriculum: Back to the Three Rs in the Maintained Schools

The debate over what knowledge is of the most worth and, in particular, what knowledge and beliefs schools ought to foster, is a perennial and universal one. Over the last generation the debate resolved itself more or less consistently into a contest between educational progressives, who believe that students themselves should choose what they want to learn, and educational conservatives, who seek to prescribe a common curriculum for all students and to purge other less valuable subjects from school programs they see as overcrowded by educational fads and frills. My purpose here, however, is not to retrace the details and history of that debate. A vast, impassioned and frequently eloquent literature exists on the subject to which writers from every imaginable social-theory orientation have contributed.[40]

Advocacy by educational conservatives of detailed and centralized prescription of what is to be taught in the schools, and even how, contains, however, a striking and important irony. The irony lies in an apparent contradiction of the key driving value in the overall conservative social purpose agenda which is unmistakably choice, the promotion of diversity of choice and freedom to choose in an open market.[41] I have already explored in general terms the nature of this ironic inversion of conservative principles as they are applied to the educational arena.[42] My purpose here is to sketch the particularly dramatic British case and to speculate on the degree to which the 'National Curriculum' thrust of current reform efforts in Great Britain contributes to the formation of a qualitatively different and substantially more 'privatized' arrangement for schooling than currently exists elsewhere.

Chitty traces the evolution since the mid-1970s of two basic ways of thinking in the British education arena about what schools ought to teach and how.[43] One he characterizes as the 'HMI model', principally because it grew out of the deliberations of Her Majesty's Inspectors about the need for and lack of some degree of commonality in the curricula being offered to 11--16-year-olds in English secondary schools. While members of the inspectorate felt some direction was needed and chafed at the erosion of their influence both in the schools and with the government under the decentralized LEA scheme, they also championed such progressive themes as interdisciplinary approaches to learning, the quality of the teaching *process* and education to meet the needs of individual children. In short, the common curriculum envisioned by HMI was a tempered, moderate, humanistic 'survival kit' version of the three-Rs with much room for student choice, teacher professionalism and for considerable, though not absolute, local autonomy. In Chitty's terms, it was a flexible 'common' curriculum rather than a rigidly defined 'core' of traditional subjects.[44]

The recent DES (Department of Education and Science) model reflected in several key DES papers, however, was quite another matter. While far from suggesting central prescription of the entire curriculum, the DES model of a prescribed core curriculum centered on traditional subject disciplines, was grounded much more in concerns about objectives, achievement, results, efficiency — and exams.[45] Even though the issue of a National Curriculum was a central plank in the Tory platform during the 1987 election, nothing in the DES vision of a core curriculum and little in government action or rhetoric seemed to hint at a really dramatic change in the shape of schooling in the maintained schools. As late as November 1985, Sir Keith Joseph was still talking in terms of a commitment to partnership with local authorities and teaching professionals in curriculum matters.[46]

Just what a Tory National Curriculum might look like, however, became obvious only during a perfunctory consultation process over a DES document entitled *The National Curriculum 5–16* and the subsequent tabling of an *Education Reform Bill* in 1987 which embodied the substance of that document and conferred 175 new discretionary powers directly on the Secretary of State.[47] The new National Curriculum would look, more than anything else, like the 1904 secondary school syllabus issued by the English Board of Education as a regulation under the 1902 Act which created British secondary schools. Allowing for a few relatively minor semantic changes, the program of studies embodied in the 'new' National Curriculum designed, in the words of Kenneth Baker, its chief architect, to provide 'a better education — relevant to the late-twentieth century and beyond — for all our children, whatever their ability, wherever they live, whatever type of school their parents choose for them'[48] is identical to the program of studies offered by maintained secondary schools in Britain at their inception.[49] The National Curriculum would be the basic 'grammar school' subject disciplines,[50] but these subjects would now be basic core curricula for all schools, including comprehensive schools — in short, a common core of 'basics' for all students. To put teeth into this universal curriculum, and to allow parents to readily identify and choose 'good' schools, an extensive program of testing will occur at ages 7, 11, 14 and 16. The vocational education role of the comprehensive schools will diminish even as the star of the (private) City Technology Colleges rises. To increase choice and diversity, maintained schools are openly encouraged under the *Education Reform Bill* to opt out of the public sector.

What is unmistakably clear is that the Tory National Curriculum means a uniform, standardized, curriculum focused directly on traditional subject disciplines and dominated by strong central control under direct political scrutiny. The essential question here is why? Why would a government overtly committed to private enterprise and hence seemingly to local and individual decision-making in education (as elsewhere) opt for a draconian reversion to centralized and standardized control of what is taught and how in schools? With stark directness, Dennis O'Keefe recently summarized the *laissez-faire* ideology of extreme right Tory Conservatism in education:

> All the economic successes since 1979 have come from shifting power to the consumer and trusting markets to do the rest . . .
> The Government should have considered financial changes, such as tax relief which would allow more parents effective rights of exit from the system: this would create competition and generate efficiency. The Government believes in capitalism. Why then does it favour coercive education? The surest advantage of markets is that they cannot be controlled politically.[51]

Why, then, in the face the such beliefs by those in power, an effort unparalleled in the history of British education to impose tight, centralized, politically rather than professionally or bureaucratically centred, control of what children in the maintained schools learn? Significantly, the control envisioned by the *Education Reform Bill* does not transgress the nominal public/private divide. This is a new set of marching orders for *public-sector* maintained schools and does not intrude in any way on the freedom of private schools to teach what and as they see fit. The new marching orders, moreover, include encouragement and even incentives for maintained schools to join the ranks of their freer private-sector competitors.

Imagining what the new schooling order might eventually look like demands an answer to the question of why the Tories decided to 'tighten up' so dramatically the public-sector schools at a time when everything indicates their principal preoccupation, indeed 'the central Thatcherite concept',[52] in education is privatization. Unfortunately, no simple and indisputable answer to that question exists, although some very interesting possibilities suggest themselves. I will present several theories and then construct from the two most plausible a view of a distinctively Thatcherite arrangement for schooling in terms of my basic model of privateness and publicness.

Why Standardize to Privatize?

A very simple answer is the generic one I offered in the preceding chapter.[53] Social policy conservatives no less than equalitarians or pluralists prefer to have their social purpose agendas widely supported. If mass schooling must be, then it is surely better from the Conservative viewpoint, to inculcate values, beliefs, knowledge and skills compatible with contemporary capitalism than to leave these to chance, preference or even, perhaps, to the vagaries of the marketplace. Students should grow up believing that capitalism in a democracy is meritocratic and, in particular, that schooling provides sufficient equality of opportunity that, on average at least, people in democratic societies get more or less what they earn and deserve in education and life. Thus, some degree of standardization of the public-school curriculum is valued by public policy conservatives mainly for its legitimation of existing and emerging class, gender and racial structures in society. To cast the matter in the rhetoric of critical theory, sensing an imminent legitimation crisis, the British government has opted for intensifying the sorting and indoctrinating roles of public-sector schools. In the conservative conscience, however, this imperative translates into the idea that all students need to share a common core of knowledge and beliefs in order to ensure social cohesion, a fundamental article of conservative *educational* policy thought.

Another answer to the question of why a government ostensibly committed to the idea of privatization in education might seek to standardize the curriculum of public-sector schools is simply that the Tories are a house divided on education policy — and on the social policy essence behind it. In this view, the *Education Reform Bill* is a tortured compromise between the fundamentally conflicting value orientations of two groups within the Tory camp. On the one hand, Baker's *Reform Bill* flows from the radical privatization wishes of what

Chitty describes as the 'neo-liberal' wing of the New Right in England (groups such as the Institute of Economic Affairs, the Adam Smith Institute, and the Centre for Policy Studies),[54] groups whose social purpose agenda corresponds more or less exactly with the free-market focus of what I have described as the quintessentially Conservative social purpose agenda.[55] On the other, the Bill derives from the authoritarian, centrist, socially hierarchical gospel of organizations such as the Hillgate Group, groups whose primary interest is in using government power — and hence schooling — to 'conserve' the existing social order and to 'instill respect for the family, private property and all the bodies which uphold the authority of the bourgeois state'.[56] In essence, this statist element in the New Right captures the strong-government, central control and regulation elements in the *equalitarian* social purpose agenda but does so *precisely in order to preserve the social stability of an order rooted in social and economic differences.* For this constituency in the British New Right, strong government, and publicly funded and provided schooling, become means not mainly of equalizing life or educational chances, but of preserving differences — differences of class and privilege, yes, but also differences in learning outcomes and life-chance expectations which underwrite and legitimate such divisions in society. Figure 6.1 shows how the troubled triangle of belief about proper role of the free-market, choice and the state creates the divided priorities and uneasy bedfellows suggested by figure 5.1, p. 69.

What unites neo-Liberal and neo-Conservative Tories most surely in education matters is a shared desire to wrench from local and largely independent education authorities their ability 'to corrupt the young' with ideas and values inhospitable to the existing social, moral and economic order. It is precisely this desire to exorcise radical ideology from the young and from their schools which, more than anything else, glues together this rather unlikely conservative common front in support of core curriculum — and clear, traditional values — in publicly funded education.

Unlike true neo-conservatives, conservatives with a neo-Liberal bent see a free-market as the primary and dominant goal of public policy and regard the state mainly as a means to it, while true neo-conservatives stress social order as the end with state control and the free-market, in that order of importance, as means. For equalitarians, on the other hand, choice becomes, like all other social purpose and educational policy objectives, a means toward equalizing opportunity and results across class and other social characteristics. For neo-Liberals, however, choice in education is the hand-maiden and

Figure 6.1   A troubled triangle of belief: The free-market, choice and control in social purpose and schooling

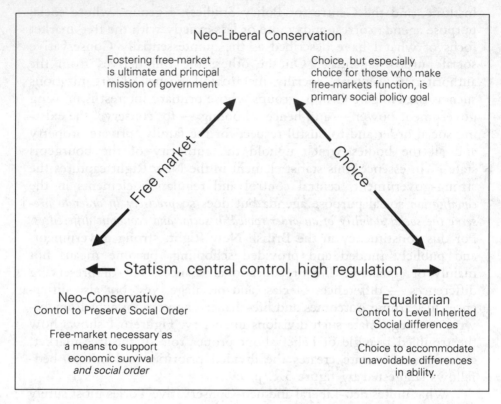

Neo-Liberal Conservation

Fostering free-market
is ultimate and principal
mission of government

Choice, but especially
choice for those who make
free-markets function, is
primary social policy goal

Free market

Choice

← Statism, central control, high regulation →

Neo-Conservative
Control to Preserve Social Order

Free-market necessary as
a means to support
economic survival
and social order

Equalitarian
Control to Level Inherited
Social differences

Choice to accommodate
unavoidable differences
in ability.

symbolic counterpart of choice in a free-market, especially choice for those most likely to contribute productively to a free-market economy.

According to this idea of a bifurcated conservative social, and educational, ideology, the Baker *Education Reform Bill* moves in contrary directions because it must satisfy Tories with many different combinations of commitment to Conservative principles, as well as to certain equalitarian principles. The privatizers, Mrs Thatcher reputedly among the more passionate,[57] demand privatization, and so the Bill, along with other recent Tory legislation, does all it can to encourage privatization in its various guises. Some of the more ardent Tory supporters of free-market schooling suggest that universal schooling itself has outlived whatever usefulness it might once have had and openly advocate abolition of compulsion and abandonment of universality in education. Tories on the neo-conservative side of the conservative spectrum, on the other hand, seek to revitalize the maintained schools by focusing their efforts on clear goals rooted in traditional educational content and practice; hence the Bill seeks to enshrine a National Curriculum directly in statute. A conflict and compromise explanation, then, could well explain the apparent contradiction in both the basic direction and the details of the educational reform efforts of the Thatcher regime.

A more disturbing possibility suggests itself, what Chitty has dubbed the 'fig-leaf' theory.[58] In this view, the real agenda is finally and completely the privatization, and deregulation, demanded by the extreme neo-Liberal right. This theory begins with the proposition that the educational policy forum is the best available political lightening rod for concern about inequality and social justice. Even a government intent on dismantling publically provided education in the long term should appear to be trying to 'equalize' the education it provides in the short term. In England, it seems increasingly clear that the extreme right now directs educational policy — and the Department of Education and Science. The whole National Curriculum undertaking could, in fact, be a political fig leaf intended to conceal the intent and ultimate consequences of a sweeping Tory privatization policy. How better, after all, to finally and completely undo a wasteful, inefficient, uncompetitive, unresponsive and unpopular public monolith than to simultaneously strangle its resources, heap draconian external regulations on it, demand program reorientations which will certainly displace many existing staff and programs (notably vocational programs and teachers) and, at the same time, provide encouragement and incentives for both schools and the most able students to exit from public-sector education? Certainly there is a powerful message about underlying long-term policy agenda in the fact that the government has not seen fit to regulate the activities of private schools.[59]

Various elements in the 1988 Act, after all, do suggest more than passingly the first step in a global phase-out of publicly operated schools. Under terms of the Act, for instance, local education authorities, *must* distribute funds to individual schools *on the basis of enrolment* at the very same time that enrolment in the maintained schools has been made 'open' in the sense that the freedom of education authorities to direct students to particular schools has been effectively removed. On reflection, such an arrangement begins to look very much like a 'soft' (incomplete, low-profile, probably introductory) version of vouchering within what are still nominally 'maintained' schools. As Chitty observes,

What was rarely questioned, however, was the essential validity of a national education system locally administered. Now the system itself is under threat; and it would appear that the 1988 Act is part of a clearly designed strategy to undermine existing structures.[60]

Furthermore, if the government has set private schools above the provisions of its new 'curriculum law', can it be for any reason other than ideological commitment to the principle that the discipline of the marketplace ensures that most private schools that survive provide high-quality programs anyway? Teachers in the private schools can be counted on to teach well what it is important to know even as students in such schools can be counted on to learn it. In the public sector, they must be ordered to do so — and many will not even then. Moreover, a positive expectation may exist in the Tory Government that public-sector teachers and students will not do so even when they are ordered to by a statutory curriculum, and therefore that, in the face of a clearly-defined National Curriculum, public-sector schools can be counted on to provide still more evidence to the public of an inability to set their own house in order.

Those most committed to the conservative social purpose agenda (what Chitty labels neo-Liberal conservatives)[61] would, as a matter of principle, want to maximize privatization of education by all available means. Within the constraints imposed by values and beliefs widely-shared among the public about equality of opportunity and an equitable distribution of educational resources, the administration has moved far and swiftly — and on many fronts — toward laying the foundations for radically privatized schooling arrangements in the United Kingdom. Surely the celerity and extent of these changes suggest considerable singleness of purpose regarding a basic future direction for English schooling — increased privatization.

From such a perspective, the 'fig-leaf' theory seems at least a plausible answer to the why-a-National-Curriculum-now question. The issue may well be conceived in slightly different terms within government and will certainly be dealt with publicly in completely different rhetoric. In the inner recesses of the Cabinet, however, the National Curriculum 'fig-leaf' may well carry the force of a rather overly generous 'last chance' for public-sector education in Britain to get its house in order. That such a 'last chance' is being provided at all, of course, rather than opting for a complete voucher system may ultimately be for no better reason than a sense that the public is not yet ready for it. Indeed, if O'Keefe's comments are at all representative of opinion close to the Prime Minister,[62] the temptation may be strong in the government to steer a long-term course for complete deregulation of education, even for a complete disengagement of government from meddling with issues of educational equity. Not long ago, electoral and opinion indications were, after all, that the Tory government might be able to think of the long-term in a way few government can. Recent discontent with the social costs of the blend of conservative doctrine, however, and especially with that ultimate neo-Liberal retreat from governmental balancing of burdens and benefits, the poll tax, has probably gone far to shorten the political horizon of Tory planning in Britain.

The conflict and compromise theory, however, serves at least equally as well as the 'fig-leaf' idea to explain the curious bifurcation of educational policy embedded in the *Reform Act*, thrusts in the seemingly contrary directions of privatization, on the one hand, and greatly increased central control of curriculum in the maintained schools on the other. It has the additional advantage of not assuming solidarity among the British Conservative Party with regard to the pre-eminence of the free-market in the hierarchy of Tory political values. Whichever explanation is accepted, the thrust of Tory educational policy after the 1987 elections seems to lead inexorably toward a qualitatively distinctive arrangement for schooling.

The Tory Private and Pseudo-Public Arena

How far public opinion and future events will allow the British Tories to go in reshaping schooling arrangements in the United Kingdom, remains to be seen. The evidence, however, points toward a desire — indeed a commitment — to go as far as possible. In short, it appears that slowing the pace of or downscaling the privatization efforts currently afoot in Britain would require something approaching a sense of political crisis. Moreover, whatever explanation of the political value origins of the National Curriculum one accepts, compelling evidence suggests that it (as well as other recent Tory educational initiatives such as relatively generous funding for the City Technology Colleges) is not aimed so much at revitalizing public-sector education as at calling it to task. Logically too, one might expect that public-sector education in England will not get a very favourable report card from a National Curriculum process whose designers include its worst enemies. Indeed, one of the primary public rationales for the massive testing program, even at the primary level, envisioned by the recent reforms is to give parents and the public a better idea of which schools are educationally productive (i.e., have children who score well on criterion-referenced tests).[63] While this approach totally ignores variations in the backgrounds of students and teachers in different schools, it does provide some measure, however crude and suspect, of the results — or at least of the easily measurable learnings that students from 'competing' schools have acquired at various stages of their education.

I assume that the Tories New Right ideologues will push British education a considerable distance down the road to a privatization quite uncommon in technologically advanced societies. The only even remotely similar arrangement I am aware of were schooling arrangements in Quebec prior to 1968, and that was clearly a very different social and political context. The New Right is unlikely, however, to have it all their way in the end. Events themselves will almost certainly reassert the equity issues within the equalitarian social purpose agenda. The recent furore over the poll tax seems likely to be just such a key equity event in the evolution of Tory social policy.

I assume, for argument's sake, however, that the Tories will succeed in making most 'controlled' schools much more private-sector-like in their governance, much more involved in a freer market in educational resources and services, and hence much more dependent on the private sector for all forms of support. They appear likely to succeed in forcing considerable, though by no means massive, defections of controlled schools from the public-sector ranks. Further, I see no reason why they will not succeed in expanding the Assisted Places Scheme into a considerably more universalistic and voucher-like system, but equally, I see no reason why they would carry it further than their own perception of the need to support 'able' students likely to contribute to British economic productivity. Complete withdrawal from the business of manipulating educational equity, at least in its fiscal representations, seems far beyond the pall of the politically supportable in Britain as elsewhere for some time to come. Attractive as the abolition of compulsory attendance is on neo-Liberal conservative ideological grounds, it is probably not going to be politically 'on' in England or anywhere else for a long time. Considerable scaling down of the length and ambit of compulsory schooling, however, is a definite possibility.

What kind of schooling arena would result from such a policy direction? How would such an arena look in terms of the basic provision, funding and regulation model I proposed in Chapter 4? Despite the National Curriculum, the very success of the Tories' multifaceted privatization efforts will probably wrest more and more students, teachers, programs, and classrooms from direct government control. Put otherwise, private and corporate control will replace attempted or real government control. On balance, despite the 'fig leaf' (or compromise with neo-conservative centralization), a long-term Tory educational future appears to mean less regulation in education rather than more. The emphasis on self-provision so evident in current British educational policy is unlikely to abate. More, not less, of the costs of schooling will be borne by individuals and private enterprise. Hence funding will be, in the aggregate, more private than at present. Finally, the balance of provision will swing markedly toward the private end of the spectrum. Just how far, however, will become increasingly difficult to determine as public-sector schools are made more private-like. In terms of figure 4.5, p. 56, the kind of schooling arrangements which might emerge from long-term application of the principles underlying current educational policy-making in Britain appear to be those in options 22 and 23. In the unlikely event that privatization should be pushed to the ultimate extreme of complete private provision and funding with no government imposed compulsion to attend school, option 16 would best represent this polar extreme (one of the two absolute poles in figure 4.3, p. 54). If all public funding were ultimately withdrawn but not all public provision, the result would be an option 17 or 18 environment in which the government still provides some programs or schools, but on a cost-recovery basis. Since it is unlikely that educational equity will disappear as a major issue from the British political arena, the farthest limits of Tory privatization may well be an option 22 or option 23 solution in which some public funding is combined with considerable private provision. The crucial issue in these options is universality, the degree to which *all* parents could access public educational funds and in what relationship to their ability to pay for the education of their children.

If the future of public funding in Britain involves extension of the Assisted Places Scheme, public funding to attend private schools will be available to to a larger group of academically able students. The capital question, of course in such a policy direction, is the degree to which funding restraint and government efforts to make the maintained schools more dependent on private resources will impinge on whatever right to a minimum quality education students in British controlled schools currently have. If Assisted Places were ultimately generalized into a complete voucher system, then all parents would presumably have a wider field of choice, although the issue of who

---

The Public and Pseudo-Private Arena

Provision: Mixed public and nominally private provision.
Funding: Public for publicly operated systems, variable mix for private schools, although the public contribution is significant.
Regulation: Moderate to high for public schools. Varies with proportion of public funding for private schools.

For the Conservative Agenda:
  + Enhanced choice and competition because many publicly funded schools are accessible to all or more students.
  − With public funding-and some degree of public provision-all the evils of government control and interference are revisited.
For the Equalitarian Agenda:
  + Some, many, most or even all private schools become subject to government regulation and thus fiscal and educational equalization measures can include 'private' schools
  − Private schools are allowed to exist and to foster differences among young people-especially differences in beliefs, values and culture — and to do so, in part at least, at the public expense.

---

would make wise choices given this greater freedom remains un-answered. Only some scheme for underwriting the expenses of a minimum quality education for *all* students whose parents cannot pay such expenses themselves will give *all* children and their parents even formal access to the benefits of increased choice in a freer educational market. Moreover, the possibility of universal, compulsory attendance at any age level hinges directly on such public funding being available to all — at the very least, to all who lack the means to pay the cost of a minimum acceptable quality education for their children.

If even the less radical changes suggested in the last few paragraphs occur in Britain, what results will be much closer to the conservative ideologue's dream, and the equalitarian's nightmare, than anything currently discernable or evolving elsewhere. Yet even this private and pseudo-public arena will offer a few consolations to the equity conscious. While it will clearly favour students, parents and entrepreneurs with the means, information and wits to play the educational market profitably, it retains some modicum of formal equality of access at least for 'able' students. However beleaguered, impoverished and emptied of talented students publicly operated schools might become, they would at least be there for those who could get nothing better. All of this is, to be sure, cold consolation for the equalitarian ideologue, but it is perhaps better from that perspective than complete disengagement of the government from the whole business of education and its regulation.

Conclusion

Just what the brave new world of British education will look like at the turn of the century is, of course, impossible to predict. Available evidence, however, suggests a strong determination on the part of the Tory government to make British education conform more closely to the tenets of the conservative social purpose agenda.[64] The course they are charting is unmistakably toward supporting and strengthening private schools, and away from increased public provision and funding. They are charting this course fundamentally because they believe that private schools are better than public-sector schools, and will always be so, since private schools must ultimately respond to market demand. Howevermuch such a belief may ignore the realities of who goes to school, where, and for what reasons, the 1987 electoral success of Thatcher's Tories suggests that it does capture a powerful public sentiment against public-sector education.

Prior to that election the Tories, after all, had created the Assisted Places Scheme out of the ashes of the defunct and little-used Direct Grant Scheme. They had set in motion a fiscal strangulation of public-sector schools at the same time that they were encouraging diverse forms of private-sector participation in the provision of educational resources and services in public-sector schools. The direction and intent was clear for all to see. While it is true that Thatcher's government ran in 1987 with some sort of national curriculum as a major plank in its election platform, the National Curriculum eventually incorporated in the *Education Reform Bill* may be much less of an attempt to fix the maintained schools than to demonstrate clearly and finally that they don't work — or at least that many of them don't — and to single out the 'ineffective' ones for all to see and avoid. Such an approach obviously ignores vast differences in pupil and parental characteristics and aspirations among different public-sector schools and especially between public comprehensive schools and fee-charging private schools. It does, however, have an attractive simplicity, and for that reason, a visceral political appeal.

In response to the recent furore over the relative quality of public and private education in the United States, Alexander and Pallas noted that, 'when good students go to good schools',[65] we cannot know which is responsible for the good performance that is likely to result. Two converse propositions seem equally certain. When poor students go to poor schools, we cannot say which is responsible for their poor performance, and to what degree. Both, in fact, probably 'cause' each other to some extent (poor students cause poor schools cause poor students) although they are part of a web of causality that is infinitely complex and extends far beyond the school. The other converse proposition is that poor students, even in outstanding schools, will not do as well as good students (in Bernstein's terms,[66] those with the cultural capital to thrive at the school game) in the same schools. Despite mountains of research, we still see but through a glass darkly the causes of what we define as quality education.[67] It is, therefore, both possible, and politically profitable, to assign the blame for social inequities to low quality public-sector schools. Who, after all, will come forward with evidence intelligible, interesting and credible to the general public that schools don't cause social and economic inequities? More to the point, perhaps, who would pay to popularize such evidence?

If the 'fig-leaf' interpretation of the National Curriculum is closest to the truth — or even only if the neo-Liberal champions of the free, market in education eventually carry the day — the Tories will inevitably, in due course, find the results of their National Curriculum and its barrage of public-sector testing quite disappointing. And in that disappointment, they will find justification for pushing ahead on all fronts with their privatization offensive. The ultimate sense behind the strange combination of standardization and privatization probably lies in the usefulness of standardization as a stepping-stone toward further privatization. Unless slowed dramatically or reversed by unforseen developments, this juggernaut can only end in an unfamiliar hybrid arrangement for schooling, in something similar to a mixed private and pseudo-public arena.

Notes

1 Tony Edwards, John Fitz, and Geoff Whitty, 'Private schools and public funding: A comparison of recent policies in England and Australia', *Comparative Education*, 21 (March 1985), p. 29.
2 Donald Fisher, 'Family choice and education: Privatizing a public good', in *Family Choice in Schooling*, ed. Michael Manley-Casimir (Toronto: D.C. Heath and Company, 1981), p. 204.
3 Janet Maw, 'National curriculum policy: Coherence and progression', in *The National Curriculum*, ed. Denis Lawton and Clyde Chitty (London: Billing and Sons, 1988), p. 60.
4 See p. 78.
5 For a summary of the distinctive features of the Scottish public education

arrangements, I am indebted to an unpublished report on sectarian schooling arrangements prepared by Stephen Lawton in 1985.

6   See p. 75.
7   Jonh P. Parry, *The Provision of Education in England and Wales* (London: George Allen and Unwin Ltd., 1971), pp. 88–96.
8   Two major systems of commercial examination boards have competed with each other in England and Wales. One, the Certificate of Secondary Education (CSE), has included a vast array of locally produced syllabus material and both boards are regionally organized. Of course, the proposal to create a single universal exam while retaining the former two-part structural organization, is part of the plan for much extended central determination and control of what is taught in the schools — including the primary schools. See, especially Roger Murphy, 'A changing role for examination boards', in *GCSE: Examining the New System*, ed. Tim Horton (Cambridge: Harper and Row, 1987), pp. 1–11; and Walter Roy, 'The Teacher Viewpoint', in *GCSE: Examining the New System*, ed. Tim Horton (Cambridge: Harper and Row, 1987), pp. 12–17.
9   James Murphy, *Church, State and Schools in Britain, 1800–1970* (London: Routledge & Kegan Paul, 1971), p. 125.
10 See p. 8.
11 Richard Pring, 'Privatization in Education', *Journal of Education Policy*, 2 (December 1987), p. 289. Also see p. 8.
12 Pring, 'Privatization in Education', *op cit.*, p. 298.
13 Geoffrey Walford, 'How dependent is the independent sector?' *Oxford Review of Education*, 13 (September 1987), p. 276.
14 Pring, 'Privatization in Education', *op cit.*, p. 297.
15 *Ibid.*
16 Pring, 'Privatization in Education', *op cit.*, especially, p. 290.
17 *Ibid.*, p. 291.
18 *Ibid.*, p. 296.
19 *Ibid.*
20 For further discussion of fiscal and educational equity issues in education, see p. 13.
21 Walford, 'How dependent is the independent sector?' *op cit.*, p. 287.
22 For an impassioned critique of the tax-expenditure theory, see William D. Burt, 'The new campaign for tax credits: 'Parochiaid' misses the point', in *Family Choice in Schooling*, ed. Michael Manley-Casimir (Toronto: D.C. Heath and Company, 1981), p. 165.
23 Walford, 'How dependent is the independent sector?' *op cit.*, p. 293.
24 *Ibid.*, p. 278.
25 *Ibid.*, p. 266–7.
26 *Ibid.*, p. 276.
27 *Ibid.*, p. 277.
28 *Ibid.*, p. 278.
29 For a clear explanation and an interesting illustration of this line of

thought, see Tony Edwards, John Fitz, and Geoff Whitty, 'Private schools and public funding: A comparison of recent policies in England and Australia', *Comparative Education*, 21 (March 1985), p. 34.

30   Walford, 'How dependent is the independent sector?' *op cit.*, p. 281–3.

31   *Ibid.*, p. 286.

32   Leonard Cantor, 'The role of the private sector in vocational education and training: The case of Japan's special training schools', *The Vocational Aspect of Education*, 39 (August 1987), p. 35.

33   *Ibid.*

34   Chitty reports that of 1800 firms approached to participate in the development of CTCs up to 1989, fewer than twenty responded positively, and even in Nottingham where a joint CTC project is scheduled, the private share will be only £1.4 million as against £9.05 million for the government. The CTCs have come under increasing fire as examples of a simple give-away of public resources to nominally private institutions. See Clyde Chitty, *Towards a New Education System: The Victory of the New Right?* (London: Falmer Press, 1989), p. 223.

35   Walford, 'How dependent is the independent sector?' *op cit.*, p. 286.

36   Information and case discussed by Richard Aldrich, 'The national curriculum debate in England: An historical perspective' (Paper presented at Faculty of Education, University of Western Ontario, London, Ontario, 27 October 1988).

37   Cited in Chitty, *Towards a New Education System: The Victory of the New Right?*, *op cit.*, p. 218.

38   The creation of the City Technology Colleges was one of the first initiatives announced by Kenneth Baker after he succeeded Sir Keith Joseph as Education Secretary in 1986. *Ibid.*, pp. 199–200.

39   See p. 15; and Figure 5.1, p. 69.

40   See, among many others, John Dewey, *Democracy and Education* (1916; reprint, New York: Macmillan, 1964), pp. 69–99; John Dewey, *Education Today* (1940; reprint, Westport, Conn.: Greenwood, 1977), pp. 273–9; Mortimer Adler, *The Paedia Proposal: An Educational Manifesto* (New York: MacMillan Publishing Company, 1982), pp. 15–36; The National Commission on Excellence in Education, *A Nation at Risk* (Cambridge, Mass: USA Research), pp. 69–76; H. Howard Russel, 'What progress in education? Review of *Progress in Education* by Nigel Wright,' *Curriculum Inquiry*, 12 (Spring 1982), pp. 105–114; Mark Holmes, 'Progress or progressive decline? A response to Howard Russel's review of *Progress in Education* by Nigel Wright', *Curriculum Inquiry*, 12 (Winter 1982), pp. 419–32; and for a recent taste of the same debate in Third World nations, Lynn Davies, 'Alternatives in education from the Third World', in *Alternative Educational Futures*, ed. Clive Harber, Roland Meigham, and Brian Roberts (London: Holt, Rinehart and Winston, 1981), pp. 63–77.

41   See p. 8.

42 See p. 68.

43 Clyde Chitty, 'Two models of a national curriculum: Origins and interpretation', in *The National Curriculum*, ed. Denis Lawton and Clyde Chitty (London: Billing and Way, 1988), pp. 34–48.

44 Chitty, *Towards a New Education System: The Victory of the New Right?*, *op cit.*, pp. 106–28.

45 Chitty, 'Two models of a national curriculum: Origins and interpretation', *op cit.*, p. 35.

46 Janet Maw, 'National curriculum policy: Coherence and progression?' in *The National Curriculum*, ed. Denis Lawton and Clyde Chitty (London: Billing and Way, 1988), p. 56.

47 Maw, 'National curriculum policy: Coherence and progression', *op cit.*, p. 58.

48 Department of Education and Science Press Release 343/87, 'The Education Reform Bill', 20 November as quoted in Klaus Wedell, 'The national curriculum and special educational needs', in *The National Curriculum*, ed. Denis Lawton and Clyde Chitty (London: Billing and Way, 1988), p. 111.

49 Richard Aldrich, 'The national curriculum: An historical perspective', in *The National Curriculum*, ed. Denis Lawton and Clyde Chitty (London: Billing and Way, 1988), pp. 22–3.

50 Aldrich's comparison of the 1904 and 1987 curricula is indeed 'instructive'.

1904	1987
English	English
Mathematics	Mathematics
Science	Science
History	History
Geography	Geography
Foreign Language	Modern Foreign Language
Drawing	Art
Physical Exercise	Physical Education
Manual Work/Housewifery	Technology
	Music

Only music is added and the only other significant change appears to be that Modern Foreign Language does not include Latin, see Richard Aldrich, 'The national curriculum', *op cit.*, pp. 22–3.

51 Dennis O'Keefe in *The Times Educational Supplement*, 18 September 1987 as quoted in Maw, 'National curriculum policy: Coherence and progression', *op cit.*, pp. 61–2.

52 M. Warnock, *A Common Policy for Education* (Oxford: Oxford Univer-

sity Press, 1988), p. 173 as quoted in Chitty, *Towards a New Education System: The Victory of the New Right?*, *op cit.*, p. 197.

53 See p. 68 and following.

54 Chitty, *Towards a New Education System: The Victory of the New Right?*, *op cit.*, p. 214.

55 See p. 8.

56 *Ibid.*, p. 214.

57 See, for instance, Maw, 'National curriculum policy: Coherence and progression', *op cit.*, p. 62.

58 Chitty, 'Two models of a national curriculum: Origins and interpretation', *op cit.*, p. 45. Chitty has since abandoned this theory in favour of the 'divided-house' explanation just described. Personal communication, 20 April 1990 and *Towards a New Education System: The Victory of the New Right?*, *op cit.*, pp. 212–15.

59 With the single exception, perhaps, of its power to allow or disallow a private school to participate in the Assisted Places Scheme.

60 Chitty, *Towards a New Education System: The Victory of the New Right?*, *op cit.*, p. 220.

61 *Ibid.*, pp. 212–13.

62 See p. 105.

63 The enhanced testing program will also, of course, make schools able to sort and stream children more 'reliably' at an earlier age.

64 See p. 8.

65 Kern Alexander and Aaron Pallas, 'Private schools and public policy: New evidence on cognitive achievement in public and private schools', *Sociology of Education*, 56 (October 1983), p. 170.

66 Basil Bernstein, *Class, Codes and Control* (London: Routledge and Kegan Paul, 1971), vol. 1, pp. 170–87.

67 I have recently reviewed, synthesized and critiqued the literature on educational quality in a paper I presented at a conference co-sponsored by the Social Sciences and Research Council of Canada and the American Education Finance Association, see Jerry Paquette, 'The quality conundrum: Assessing what we cannot agree on', in *Scrimping or Squandering?: Financing Canadian Schools*, ed. Stephen Lawton and Rouleen Wignall (Toronto: OISE Press, 1989), pp. 11–28.

Chapter 7

Issues in Conflict:
The Principal Arguments

Many governments, not just the British, are actively wrestling with the merits of and the means for further privatization of schooling arrangements, although none has gone as far in establishing a comprehensive mélange of policies favouring privatization.[1] In the United States, the technicalities and legal implications of various voucher and tax-credit schemes are subjects of perennial debate. In Canada, half the provinces have already developed funding formulae for eligible private schools and the issue has recently been hotly debated before and studied by a government commission in Ontario. Controversy over the relative merits of more versus less private responsibility, initiative and entrepreneurship in education is alive and well in a wide range of countries — and not just among members of GATT or even only among relatively prosperous nations. According to Steven Heyneman of the World Bank, the major educational strategy being recommended to debt-ridden Third World countries is to concentrate on quality rather than quantity, that is, to abandon their attempts at universality and privatize their schools.[2]

Ultimately each side in the 'to privatize or not to privatize' debate draws arguments from its own fundamental assumptions about social purpose, from its particular concept of what society ought to be, and about how it can come closer to such a state of affairs. Specific arguments and issues about schooling arrangements are grounded in basic beliefs about the nature of the common good, about the best type of human society possible within the realities of the human condition. Occasionally these underlying principles undergo some strange transformations and mutations in the private versus public schooling debate, but they are always there, providing the final *raison d'être* for the specific issues and arguments various protagonists employ in the debate.

No ultimate issue or decisive argument, however, looms on the horizon — in Britain or anywhere else in the non-communist world — for either privatization or a monolithic public monopoly in education. Instead, tension among competing views of social purpose raises a panoply of issues and arguments that allows little certainty. In the end, this mélange of issues throws protagonists, participants and observers back on their own beliefs and convictions — and on their own interpretations of available evidence. From these value-driven interpretations, all the players in the schooling drama judge how well or poorly current schooling arrangements serve children, parents, educators, the common good as they perceive it and, not least, the demands of economic competitivity in an increasingly high-tech, information-based international marketplace.

My intent here is to marshall and examine the principal arguments, on the one hand, for extending private provision and funding and for decreasing government regulation in education and, on the other, for extending public provision and funding and increasing government regulation in education. My intent is not, however, to take a stand for one position or the other. In the final analysis, I believe that no narrowly focused social purpose agenda encompasses all that should be striven for in human affairs and public policy. Fundamentally, public policy-making is complex and conflicted, not because we have yet to discover the best orchestration of human affairs, but because there *is no* 'best' way of doing things in all places and times. If there were, and if we could come to know it, we would, in effect, obviate the need for a political process to change and refine our efforts at public policy-making. In particular, it seems very doubtful that, under any circumstances, either a completely privatized and deregulated schooling arena or a tightly controlled public monopoly[3] — or close approximations to either — would well serve the public good conceived as the greatest good of the greatest number. For a variety of reasons as well, it seems equally doubtful that either polar extreme would well serve the long-term interests of those who contribute most visibly to economic productivity in technologically advanced societies.

No final truths here, then, no clear pronouncement on some ideal arrangement. Instead, what I offer is a review of generic issues and arguments surrounding the private/public school debate and commentary on them. Beyond that, each reader must decide which arguments and issues should predominate in any particular time and place, and, consequently, what mix of public and private provision, and what degree of government regulation, is desirable and politically feasible. Finally, I have said little about the advent of a social purpose agenda driven mainly by the tenets of structural pluralism since I introduced it in chapter 2.[4] An increasingly important factor in deciding what mix of provision, funding and regulation best serves the public good is the cultural and linguistic mix that makes up that public. The 'ethnic' factor looms ever larger on the political horizons of politicians and policy-makers confronted with large minorities who vote minority issues in local and regional elections. I believe, however, that the sensible approach is to examine the generic issues and arguments — the task of this chapter — and then deal with the impact of the emerging pluralist agenda on them — the task of the following chapter.

Pandora's Box: The Cases For and Against Private Education

The debate between advocates of increased and decreased privatization crystallizes around certain key claims and counterclaims. Among them are claims and counterclaims about the effects of various alternative methods for enhancing privatization without undermining the major equity rationales for publicly funded and regulated education.

Case 1

Claim

> *Schooling is about the transmission and inculcation of values, culture and beliefs more than about cognitive knowledge, indeed the selection of what is to be learned is inescapably grounded in values. No homogeneous public system can well serve the divergent value preferences and orientations in a complex, pluralistic society.*

The real competition among schools, and especially between public and private schools, is over values. It is precisely Horace Mann's vision of the common school as shaper of uniform values and beliefs for homogeneous, steady-state democracies that is the worst condemnation of publicly provided and closely regulated schooling.[5] Public schools are everybody's and consequently they are nobody's. Value-free education is a dangerous delusion and a self-contradiction. Education is the inculcation of values and beliefs even more than the imparting of knowledge. All attempts to find widely agreed-upon values and beliefs which can be actively fostered by all schools have failed both in the past and the present.

Quality education is in the eye of the beholder. What is needed is the freedom for parents and pupils to choose schools that reflect their most important beliefs and values: not a monolithic public system which plies captive students with a fragmented and inconsistent mix of secular, humanist principles and ends by selling indifference to all values as the chief characteristic of the educated person. The greatest danger to human societies is not cultural fragmentation and loss of social cohesion, but abandonment of the very idea of right and wrong, good and evil. Let those who wish their children to be imbued with liberal humanism send their children to schools founded on such a belief structure. Let those, however, who want their children to partake deeply of their ancestral cultures and languages have schools that foster these cultures and languages, so long as such schools also provide a firm grounding in the common national culture within which these children must live and work. Let those who believe in the unique character-building power of elitist schools have them[6]; and let those who wish progressive schools with flexible standards have what they want as well.

In increasingly pluralistic, multicultural and multilingual national societies, it becomes less and less likely that public schools can be all things to all people. They should stop trying and recognize the contribution to education and human development made by schools established to help children maintain and enrich their cultural or religious identity. Such schools need not be, and rarely are, isolated enclaves of educational regressivism, although some are forced into such a posture by the ostracism they experience at the hands of public education officials and systems. How many minority parents would, in any case, choose to send their children to a school which prepared children for life in their ancestral society rather than for life in their host society? The sad irony — and the main subject of the following chapter — is that public systems seeking to assimilate minorities by replacing their cultures and languages have a very poor track record internationally of adequately preparing minorities for full participation in their host societies and economies.

Counterclaim

> *On the inculcation of a common core of values and beliefs rests the very survival of a society. In modern societies only schools can ensure*

*sufficient sharing of principles, convictions and knowledge to provide
a basis for social cohesion and economic efficiency.*

Without the common school as guarantor of a common socialization
among culturally and socially diverse elements in society, the future
can offer only social fragmentation, economic disaster and, in the end,
political anarchy. Shared beliefs and knowledge are the foundation of
every national society and we cannot live together harmoniously and
productively if we allow a large proportion of our young to attend
schools that make us ever more different from one another in our
beliefs and basic knowledge. The surest way to bring about social and
economic apocalypse is to hive off students from one another on the
basis of social class, gender, ethnicity, ability or religion. This is
exactly what most private schools do.[7]

The impact of mass media, especially television, makes the
socialization and enculturation role of the common school more
important than ever. Young people today are assaulted as never before
with a barrage of conflicting value messages, many of them inimical
to the most basic principles of human decency, respect for self and
others, and peaceful and purposeful co-existence. In such a world, the
school must be at the front-line of efforts to imbue the young with
shared beliefs and knowledge which make social harmony and economic productivity a possibility. Only schools subject to public scrutiny
and regulation can be entrusted with this vital task.

Case 2

Claim

*The common school is a myth. It has never existed and is probably
farther from realization today than ever. Social cohesion is better
served where parents and pupils make conscious choices from among
real alternatives in the values, knowledge and beliefs purveyed by
competing schools.*

The most élitist schools of all are public, not private. All private
schools provide some scholarship aid for needy and able students.
Except in jurisdictions with 'in-house' (i.e., public-sector) vouchering
or court-imposed busing, students are usually compelled to attend the
nearest publicly supported school offering a suitable program, generally

the neighbourhood elementary or secondary school. Despite fiscal equalization, which is never complete, children in high tax-capacity neighbourhoods and regions experience the benefits of very high per-pupil spending while those in low tax-capacity areas experience the consequences of very low per-pupil spending. They have no choice in the matter. Poor children never go to public schools in rich neighbourhoods. They do, however, sometimes go to 'élite' private schools.

Nor does having the majority of students in a geographical area in the same system, or even under a common roof, provide any guarantee that they experience the same curriculum or receive the same messages about what values count in life and society. Critical theorists are quick to point out that academic and non-academic stream students exist not only in different worlds of knowledge, but in categorically opposed worlds of belief about themselves, their significance as human beings and what they ought to do and expect in society and the workplace. In the same 'common' public school system, often under the same roof, members of one group learn that they are persons of worth who can and will accomplish important things in life through creative and divergent thinking, and furthermore that they will be richly rewarded for doing so. The other much larger group learns to obey, refrain from criticism and critical thought, and endure any required amount and degree of occupational and social boredom.[8] If public schools were delivering on their mandate to provide a common good quality education and uniform value orientations to all students, they would not be plagued with drug and alcohol abuse, violence, lack of discipline, widespread student apathy, alienated teachers and high drop-out rates.

A society of clones is, in any case, a hideous prospect. The best assurance we have of a vital and humane society is not in pretending to give everyone the same knowledge and values in public education systems that, in fact, are radically stratified by race, class and gender, but in fostering and facilitating informed and conscious choice among viable alternatives. So long as some minimal regulation is in place to avoid the propagation and institutionalization of hate and violence, we should strive for educational arrangements that work toward a cohesive diversity rather than an impossible and inhuman sameness. From this point of view, the 'common curriculum' enthusiasts (and especially advocates of a narrow core of traditional subjects) invite even further alienation from learning in general and schooling in particular by their efforts to force everyone into the same learning and value molds.

Voluntarism is a far more potent educational motivator than compulsion. In a world where both private and public return on educational investment below the post-secondary level (except in Third World countries), and outside of certain types of programs, is ever more questionable, it makes eminently good sense to increase choice and diminish compulsion in schooling.

Counterclaim

> *Public education has done very well indeed in both its educational and its social mandate. Without some version of the common school, society as we know it would quickly disintegrate into a babel of languages, life styles, values and beliefs so diverse that social and economic anarchy would be the inevitable results.*

For all the faults and demonstrable inequities in current arrangements for the public provision of education, these arrangements serve the cause of social and economic cohesion far better than a free-market ever could. The solution to inequities in public systems is not to do away with public provision, but to redesign and refine it so that it provides more equal access, opportunity, treatment and results. Adequate allowances for cultural, linguistic and value divergence can and should be made within public education — not in spite of it. Only by doing so will we ensure a core of shared knowledge and beliefs essential for societal survival and economic productivity. Public schools, and only public schools, can ensure that we remain peoples sufficiently at peace with one another to engage in socially and economically constructive action.

Public education in North America has demonstrated its capacity to cope with the problem of quantity by increasing dramatically since World War II the proportion of young people who complete a secondary-level education certificate. The European systems have demonstrated their ability to produce high quality education in the public sector, although with much greater selectivity. What is needed is to improve both the quantity and quality of public education, not supplant it. The best way to accomplish this is to promote more, not less, common learning. Social cohesion and economic productivity are a sufficient charter for public education and for a common core of universal, compulsory subjects for all students except those with severe learning handicaps. A universally better educated society is also a more economically productive and competitive society.

Case 3

Claim

> *Public education is a disastrous squandering of scarce resources on an incurably inefficient form of schooling.*

In Brimelow's terms:

> The prevailing orthodoxy in American pedagogy is umbilically connected with that section of the country's political culture that naturally thinks in terms of equity and social reform rather than economic efficiency.[9]

In terms strongly reminiscent of West's scathing generic attack on publicly provided education,[10] Brimelow denounces the public *provision* of education in the United States as 'the American version of Soviet agriculture, beyond help as currently organized because its incentive structure is all wrong'.[11] Specifically, Brimelow and like-minded critics of *publicly provided* education charge that it results in:[12]

1 a 'persistent tendency to treat capital as a free good and all possible uses of it as equal';
2 'constant mismatching of supply and demand';
3 'prices administered without regard to incentives, so that all teachers must be paid on the same scale'; and
4 'an absence of internal checks and balances to prevent whole-sale imposition of officially favoured enthusiasms . . .'[13]

In short, publicly provided education is incurably inefficient and no amount of regulation, manipulation or restructuring will redeem it from that vice. Only competition in a freer educational market can.

Counterclaim

> *The putative efficiency of private schools is an illusion. It is based on the tendency of private schools to offer narrowly academic programs which are much less expensive than the technical and vocational programs public systems offer. Public systems must accept all students, including those with handicaps and problems that make serving them very expensive. Private schools are free to reject expensive-to-serve*

students. Above all, this imaginary efficiency is purchased by under-paying and overworking private school teachers.

Private schools are not intrinsically more efficient than public schools. Despite various studies purporting to demonstrate superior overall performance among private school students, such studies inevitably compare apples and oranges.[14] First, private schools can select their students. Public systems, on the other hand, must take all who come to them, including the hard-to-serve (who are invariably also expensive-to-serve) and a large proportion of students who choose very expensive vocational programs and courses. Second, the students who enrol in private schools are typically different in many important respects from their public school counterparts. At the least, they come from families who value education sufficiently to bear the cost and inconvenience of sending their children to a private school. They are often, although not always,[15] young people whose parents have provided them with a richness and diversity of experience altogether lacking to many of those in, or headed toward, 'vocational', 'occupational' or 'basic' level tracks or streams in public systems.

The fiscal advantage of the right to refuse admission that is enjoyed by private schools has increased greatly recently with the proliferation of special education legislation compelling public schools to provide an *appropriate* education for *every* school-age child within their jurisdiction. Unlike private schools that provide mainly academic programs to motivated, relatively capable students, public schools are required to provide a wide variety of programs for students of varied backgrounds, interests and abilities. The present inefficiency of public schooling is, in part at least, a direct result of the success of public policy aimed at making the public schools more accessible to more pupils. In Burt's terms:

> The public schools' high retention rate of socially and learning-handicapped children is the result of their own policy-determined attempts to make mainstream education attractive and useful to pupils who in the past would have been grouped together in classes for retarded or delinquent students.[16]

Whether this is good or bad depends on where one's view of social purpose leads on the subject of mainstreaming disadvantaged and handicapped students, but one thing is abundantly evident, mainstreaming policies of all sorts result in very high marginal costs in public systems, marginal costs which are not shared by most private schools. This is so even though private education can be and often is very expensive on a per-pupil basis.

Finally, the 'efficiency' of private schools has been very much a product of the ability and willingness of private schools to attract teachers who were willing to work for wages considerably below those paid to their counterparts in the public schools. In the case of religiously based schools, especially Roman Catholic private or parochial schools, teachers have often worked for subsistence or below subsistence wages to further the cause of schools reflecting and pro-pagating their religious beliefs. In Roman Catholic schools through-out the world, extensive use has been made of members of religious orders who were quite willing to work for subsistence wages, wages which, in any case, they merely contributed to the common revenues of their order. So important was such 'teacher subsidy' that the recent and considerable decline in the number of young people entering religious orders has provoked a major crisis in Catholic education in jurisdictions where Catholic schools were (and sometimes still are) receiving little or no public funding.[17] Catholic schools have dealt with that crisis in various ways. The preferred method has been to access public funds. Where that has failed, increased tuition fees have helped defray the cost of moving teacher salaries closer to a living wage.[18]

The ultimate question posed by educational efficiency purchased with bargain-basement teacher salaries is that of how well teachers can be expected to teach when they work for a pittance. Is it wise to entrust the education of children to teachers whose salaries and working conditions make them an oppressed class? Can one attract talented and motivated people into a teaching profession whose salary levels are far below what such a person might earn in other careers? Grave dangers to educational quality lie behind policies, including enhanced competition in a freer schooling market, which result in low salaries and oppressive working conditions for teachers.

More fundamentally, the argument that more competition in schooling will contribute to the public good is deeply suspect. School-ing is not like selling hamburgers. The improvement of schools requires long-term planning — not mercurial change to meet passing fads. All children count, not just those of parents who know how to play the school game to win.[19] Basic considerations of liberty and human dignity dictate that schooling should be, to a considerable degree, insulated from the market.[20] To trust schooling entirely to the vagaries of a free-market is to invite a social stratification even more rigid and impermeable than what we already have. If public schools do not do so, who will work to equalize the educational and life chances of those with little 'cultural capital' and with families that have very low aspirations for them? Surely not private schools whose principal concern is to sell their product in a market which favours those who can convince parents that they provide an inside track to school and career success.

Case 4

Claim

At the heart of private schools' ability to provide high-quality education is their right to control access.

If vouchers or tax credits enlarge the demand for private school places at public expense, the question of how such schools select — and reject — students inevitably becomes subject to public scrutiny and government regulation. Where public funding under any guise is provided to private schools, only the most minimal regulation should be tolerated. Anything more than the most basic constraints should be avoided. Governments should avoid prescribing any more than that private schools receiving direct or indirect benefits should avoid propagating hatred against identifiable groups in society and should show some minimal evidence of stability over time (the criteria currently used for lower level public funding eligibility in British Columbia). Especially to be avoided is interference in the selection procedures private schools use to determine who is admitted. Access control is an indispensable key to quality control in the private schools. Furthermore, control of access is the only way to maintain the distinctive religious or moral character of education offered in private schools, in short, the only means to preserve their very *raison d'être*. If public funding reduces price rationing as a form of access control available to private schools, they must nonetheless remain free to determine their own admission standards and requirements without government meddling.

Regulation and public funding, after all, are not unrelated variables. Wherever governments have provided funding to private schools, they have always introduced some form of regulation. If public funding is to be used to stimulate private education and enlarge access to it, some regulation of funded private schools is inevitable. If such funding is to lead to a freer educational market and real choice for more parents, young persons and adult learners, the urge to regulate must be resisted.

A freer educational market is the best defense we can have against educational quackery. Certainly the track record of publicly provided education does not inspire confidence that it enjoys some peculiar immunity to pedagogical and policy charlatanism.[21] In the last two decades, sociologists from many countries have presented abundant statistical evidence that current forms of public schooling 'don't make a difference' for students from lower socioeconomic backgrounds.[22] In response, public schools have rushed from one impotent panacea to another to prove to the governments that support them that they can and will make a difference in the educational and life chances of most students. Accountability — how to demonstrate to increasingly scep-tical politicians that educational monies are being wisely spent and get results that official educational goals say they should — has been the byword of publicly provided education for at least the last decade. For all the fads, however, the more things change in public education, the more they remain the same. What the public schools have demon-strated, more than anything else, is that they cannot account for the public monies they consume; at least not in terms of their declared mission of providing *equal opportunity* to people from all classes and backgrounds to:

1   basic knowledge and skills;
2   creative expression;
3   social competence;
4   autonomy as an individual;
5   good citizenship; and
6   preparation for work.[23]

People stop buying computers that don't work well for them. They should be equally free to stop sending their children to schools that don't work well for them. The more public funding is used as a justi-fication for public regulation and control, the less freedom to choose it will offer.

Because the history of public funding of private education is riddled with intrusive government regulation (the ultimate case being the public and pseudo-private arrangement in Holland),[24] private schools, especially the best established schools with a firmly entrenched reputation of excellence, are loathe to accept any form of public support. As Gossage puts it in her illuminating account of the élite independent schools in Canada,[25] despite the enormous financial strains faced by most of them, such schools prefer to 'maintain their current status — poorer but prouder'. If governments are sincere in their desire to confer the benefits of a freer schooling market on more members of society, they can only do so by rigorously eschewing the temptation to regulate the private schooling they choose to fund.

Counterclaim

> *Public funding without public scrutiny and control is unthinkable in a free and democratic society. The principle of government accountability for use of tax revenues is fundamental and no scheme which violates it should ever be accepted by responsible government. Especially opprobrious is the idea that government should fund private schools and not have a voice in who can attend such schools.*

The slogan which, more than any other, gave birth to the American revolution was 'no taxation without representation'. To appropriate public funds for use by private organizations who are not required to account for their use is repugnant to the principles of democratic government. It is also unlikely to pass any of the tests Hall *et al.* suggest as essential for successful adoption and implementation of public policy. The proposition that government should fund private schools without regulating them is unlikely ever to appear legitimate, feasible or politically supportable to elected representatives who must answer at the polls for the taxes they spend.[26] In short, such a proposition is simply a political non-starter.

Particularly invidious is the suggestion that private schools should help themselves to the public purse and be allowed to retain arbitrary admission procedures, or procedures that favour one or more particular groups in society. If all are to pay for school X, why should only Catholic, only Baptist, only Moslem or only Chinese children attend there? Why, for that matter, should X be allowed, as a matter of choice or policy, to induct more Anglicans, more Ukrainians or more atheists than the overall proportion of the population represented by such groups? If all pay for X, at least in part, why should all not have equal access to X on an equal footing? Without some form of guaranteed access to all publicly funded private schools for all students, further privatization, especially government sponsored privatization, will increasingly turn public systems into ghettos of educational mediocrity. What will result from expanding private school enrolments at public expense are public-school ghettos catering to students of modest academic abilities and aspirations.

The solution to public schools that fail to live up to their mandate of equal access to schooling and its benefits is not to abandon them but to improve them — specifically, to improve their accountability for their primary mission, equalization of educational and life-chance opportunities. What is needed are more alternatives within the public sector — but alternatives freely accessible to all. Especially needed are tough-minded, back-to-the-basics magnet schools and efforts to implement merit as a basis for professional and financial advancement in teaching. Principals, especially, should no longer enjoy anything resembling tenure or guaranteed administrative status. The administration of schools should become more school centered, more responsive to parents through local school-level governance arrangements akin to those being encouraged by the Tory government in the UK.[27] In these and similar steps, and not in using the public purse to foster privatization of schooling, lies the possibility of making education deliver on its promise of more equal life chances for all.

Case 5

Claim

> *The right for students who meet admission criteria set by a private school to attend there is a fundamental human right grounded in the right of parents to choose the type of education their children receive, a right recognized by the Universal Declaration of Human Rights. This right must be preserved in tact in any schooling arrangement.*[28]

The right of parents to choose a private rather than a public school for their children is a direct corollary of their right to choose the type of education their children should receive. Once again, public schools are everyone's and therefore no one's. Just how serious the consequences in educational and life chances are of failing to allow parents to choose an education in harmony with their beliefs and culture is all too evident in the history of minorities that have failed to assimilate successfully into their host societies. The educational failure and marginal social and economic status of minority groups such as migrant workers and aboriginal peoples is its own proof that the assimilationist mission of universalist public education affects most cruelly those it was commissioned to help to a better life. How and why this has happened is the subject of the next chapter, but that it is so seems beyond question in light of recent research.

Counterclaim

> *The right of the rich to exit public education systems, a right given to*
> *them by the current price rationing system for controlling access to*
> *private schools, deprives public education of the support of parents*
> *most likely to work effectively to improve public education if their*
> *children had to attend public schools.*

What is most wrong with private schooling is that access to it is largely a function of ability to pay. The price rationing of private schooling ensures that the rich have a fundamental right which the poor generally do not enjoy; the right of exit from publicly provided education. Since the rich and the upper middle class are also classes of people particularly concerned about the quality of education offered to their children, the loss of substantial and growing numbers of them from the ranks of parents supporting public schools is a critical loss of concern and commitment in the public sector. Public policy should attempt to slow rather than hasten this exodus.

Case 6

Claim

> *The initiative and entrepreneurialism for most private schools comes*
> *from religious belief and strong ethical commitments. To tamper with*
> *schools that seek to foster such beliefs and commitments is to deny*
> *freedom of religion and conscience.*

At least in their early stages, most private schools are the product of a desire to foster religious belief or strong ethical or moral commitment, a commitment to academic excellence being a frequent common denominator among the moral commitments of private schools. Tampering with the freedom to found and support such schools is a denial of freedom of religion and conscience. Furthermore, to insist that rate-payers who wish to send their children to a private school support financially *both* a public school system *and* a private school is, in itself, a massive circumscription of that freedom. To further diminish the rights of private schools to exist and compete for students is to move further in the direction of a state-imposed value system and religion (or non-religion).

135

Counterclaim

> *Religion and ethics are a matter for the family and church, not for publicly-supported schools. Not only should all private schools refrain from indoctrination of students into narrow belief systems and needlessly constraining ethical principles, no public funding should reach any private schools that offer religious or moral education beyond the inculcation of habits and attitudes required to live in a free and democratic society.*

Although often couched in language that conceals the fact, this argument denies that education is inescapably, fundamentally and essentially moral action. At the very least, it seeks to identify a minimal, universal set of values which all schools should foster, and to which all schools should limit their moral indoctrination activities both overt and covert. Widespread, massive and largely unsuccessful efforts in many lands over the last decade to arrive at publicly acceptable 'values education' programs attest to just how unlikely agreement on such a minimal list of 'required' values is.

The second underlying principle of this counterclaim, that no public funding should reach programs of religious or particularistic moral indoctrination, has led to the refusal of the American Supreme Court to allow public funding of private schools under its strict interpretation of the first amendment to the American constitution prohibiting excessive entanglement of church and state.[29] Despite numerous and ingenious legislative efforts at the state and federal level to find a way around the first amendment and make public monies available to parochial schools, the American Supreme Court has consistently struck them down on the basis that, even if such monies could somehow be earmarked for the secular component of the education provided in parochial schools, the mere supervision of such arrangements by government would constitute an excessive entanglement of church and state. Nonetheless, many commentators see definite movement toward permitting such 'parochiaid' in recent judgments and believe another test case with an additional Conservative jurist on the court may finally yield a judgment favourable to public funding of religious schools in the United States.[30] Such an outcome would, of course, be in direct defiance of the principles underlying counterclaim 6.

Case 7

Claim

> *Private schools reduce public expenditures on education. Governments should acknowledge this saving by contributing to the costs of education in private schools — at least up to some amount less than or equal to what it would be required to spend on such pupils if they were in public schools.*

Private school supporters pay school taxes too. Why should they and their children be excluded from all benefit of such taxes? Even where public funds do assist private education in one form or another, the existence of private schools relieves government of educational expenditures equal to the difference between the marginal cost of accommodating in public schools all students attending private schools and the value of whatever support is provided to private schools. That difference is, almost everywhere, considerable.

Furthermore, the argument that public support of private schools bleeds public schools of resources they need and have a right to is a bogeyman precisely because public schools invariably would incur marginal costs greater than any support governments ever provide to students in private schools if those students were to attend public schools. In other words, with no change in funding formulae affecting their public school system, governments would always be worse off financially if all private school students within their jurisdiction suddenly showed up at the doors of state-operated schools. As Shipman states the case, when asked what they would do if private schools closed their doors, public school administrators invariably respond that they would 'find the money', and therefore 'the locus of schooling', not money, is the real issue.[31] Charges of savaging public systems to help private schools are smokescreens for attempts to defend public-sector power and jobs. The ultimate issue is choice, the right of parents and pupils to choose in a free educational marketplace.

Counterclaim

> *Government is under no obligation to make good the additional educational costs incurred voluntarily by parents who send their children to private schools.*

The so-called 'double-taxation' burden of private school supporters is a myth. Private school supporters have voluntarily chosen not to avail themselves of publicly provided schooling paid for from tax revenues, including their own taxes. They have the same rights to public educational services as those who attend publicly operated schools. Having freely chosen to send their children to private schools, private school supporters must bear their fair share of the cost of public education in addition to the private-school fees they pay. Only by distributing the cost of publicly funded schooling over all tax payers can high quality education be provided to all pupils, regardless of ability to pay. This principle is fundamental to all the diverse approaches to funding education in various jurisdictions. If childless couples, bachelors, widows and the retired are required to contribute to the costs of schooling, why should private school parents be exempt? In the end, everyone benefits from an educated populace and all should therefore share in the cost of public education.

Case 8

Claim

> All students and parents benefit from freer competition in the
> educational marketplace.

More competition is good for everyone. An enlightened attitude on the part of public education officials and supporters toward private schools would be one of respect and symbiotic cooperation within a pattern of friendly but dynamic competition. Competition makes everyone define goals and work hard toward them. Competition demands careful weighing of innovation and experimentation — and the courage and ability to do what parents will ultimately see as best for their children — and not just in private schools but in public schools as well. In short, competition is the best means available to make *all* schools responsive to the wishes and preferences of parents and communities. No surrogate exists for the right to leave and go to a competitor when it comes to providing a service in a consumer-pleasing and efficient manner. With competition everyone gets more of what everyone wants.

Counterclaim

> A freer educational marketplace, one in which there is some degree of
> formal equality of access to all types of schooling, will help those

*groups in society who are already most successful and further reduce
the educational and life chances of the already educationally disadvantaged.*

This ironic result flows from the fact that those who come from
backgrounds where parents, extended family and friends esteem
education and know how the schooling game is played, will make the
right choices as more choices become available. One can expect with
great certainty that more upper-class and middle-class background
parents than working-class parents will continue to make wise and
well informed choices when measured against the standards of self-
fulfilment and earning power in the future lives of their children.[32]
The Assisted Places Scheme in Britain provides an up-to-date experiment in extended choice which demonstrates that it is overwhelmingly those whose parents come from relatively high socioeconomic
status backgrounds who take advantage of the enhanced choice made
available by the plan.[33]

This is hardly new or shocking information. Indeed, in Bernstein's terms, only children from such backgrounds are likely to have
accumulated the 'cultural capital' to qualify for admission to selective
private schools in any case.[34] Only public systems have a mandate to
help children from disadvantaged backgrounds improve their educational and life-chances. To the extent that public policy weakens
publicly provided education it further weakens the life chances of
those who already have the worst prospects in school and in life.
Rather than concentrating on weakening public education, government should concentrate on making it a more effective instrument of
social policy.

Case 9

Claim

> *In the new reality of the world economy quality is more important
> than quantity in schooling, not only for the poor nations but more so
> even for the rich. Universalism in schooling should be scaled down
> and efforts focused on educating well those most likely to contribute
> positively to society and to economic competitiveness in a high-tech
> world market.*

Universal, compulsory education has always been, in any case, a
myth. High illiteracy rates in the most technically advanced nations

demonstrate clearly that current schooling arrangements result in little learning for a large portion of students who, nonetheless, have been formally in attendance at school for ten or twelve years of their lives and may even have obtained some sort of certification of their school learning. Moreover, high secondary drop-out rates may be more a symptom that young people uninterested in academic pursuits (or unlikely to succeed in them) have grasped the reality of their situation and prospects in the high-tech economy of the present and future than a social problem that can somehow be solved by government policy.

If Perrow is right, new employment opportunities in the job market of the next decade will be overwhelmingly in basic service industries where little if any formal education is required.[35] The most fundamental reality of the current world economy is that technology is replacing human labour. Moreover, the most menial and dangerous jobs are increasingly being exported to Third World nations and the remaining unskilled, semi-skilled and even highly skilled manufacturing tasks in developed nations are falling into the steely hands of robots. The ranks of lower and even middle management are being thinned steadily by advances in computer technology and software. Far from demanding universal literacy and numeracy, the new high-tech economy requires only that nations develop an élite cadre of talented, highly skilled technocrats and managers. Universal public education no longer contributes demonstrably to economic productivity — certainly not in proportion to the resource investment it requires. On the contrary, it siphons off resources which should be invested in research, high-level technical skills and capital equipment. Why then should young people who have no interest in or aptitude for higher education remain in school until late adolescence? Why should they be legally compelled to remain in school until age fifteen or sixteen? Why should they even be encouraged to do so?

In more general terms, why should public schools be compelled to accept all children, 'no matter how disinclined to learn, disruptive or burdened with physical, intellectual, or emotional disabilities'.[36] Whose good is served by this massive, extended legal compulsion in schooling — compulsion of all young persons to attend and compulsion of public school systems to accept all? Is it the good of all students — or merely the institutional aggrandisement, the empire-building tendencies of public education systems? Were we not better off when schooling was seen as a scarce resource rather than a universal birthright? Many of the most disturbing problems in public education today are directly related to compulsion, to the legal requirement to serve and be served in public schools. If young people were free to withdraw from education at an earlier age, if some particularly troubled children were exempted altogether from the requirement to attend school, everyone would be better off. Moreover, if parents were required to make some clear, *unmistakably direct* contribution to the cost of educating their own children, all parents and their children would come to see education as a resource rather than a right.

Counterclaim

All elements of national societies continue to benefit in difficult-to-measure ways from universal education. It is socially destructive in the extreme and an insupportable risk to societal and economic stability to allow whole classes of persons to enter adulthood with little or no formal education.

Universal education is a universal benefit. The fact that public schools have fallen short of the mark of universal basic literacy and numeracy is no reason for abandoning the effort but rather reason for redoubling it. Democracy and responsible government require an educated populace. Our very survival as peoples, nations and increasingly as a planet, is imperiled by political processes which confer electoral power on masses of voters who live and vote in ignorance. Totally aside from economic considerations, then, universal, compulsory education is a basic national and international survival strategy.

Bored, poverty-stricken, hungry and unfulfilled people disturb existing political and economic arrangements in dangerous and unpredictable ways. Not alcohol, not drugs, not all the cheap electronic entertainment in the world, lulls bored, frustrated and useless-feeling people into easy acceptance of their lot in life. Economic arguments notwithstanding, the common good requires universal education that can at least *offer* to all the means to some sense of self-worth and fulfilment.

Education is far more than technical skill and a good nose for the marketplace. As organizations, peoples and nations we make increasingly consequential and fateful decisions for our future — and especially for the future of our children and descendants. If we loose our commitment to a broad liberal education for the greatest possible number, we may diminish far more than the humanity of our awareness, perceptions and relations. Given the awesome power to degrade all aspects of our environment that is part of our new-found technological prowess, we may thereby seal the doom of the human race.

The real challenge of learning to live humanely with technology may be to accept that work-sharing can enrich human experience by providing meaningful and challenging work *and leisure* for more persons but, above all, to place ecological concerns in the forefront of decision-making in all areas of human life and action. Both of these policy directions require a reconceptualization of human and social purpose in less econometric terms. We may be wise to invest in more doctors, lawyers, electronic engineers and computer programmers than we would need to survive and compete effectively in the world market if every doctor, lawyer, electronic engineer and computer programmer worked flat-out all year around. We should expand, not diminish our investment in the creative and artistic expression of all the members of society, if for no other reason than that less and less of the total number of person hours of work available in society will be required to produce consumer goods. But above all, if we are to survive long on planet earth, we must all learn to put ecological questions ahead of the bottom line of our personal and corporate lives more often.

Only public education commissioned out of a mandate to the common good is likely to pick up the gauntlet of these challenges. One of the chief advantages of the market system is that it holds supply in some conformity with demand. Should we, however, — can we afford to — accept an educational market in which the supply of educational services at all levels will be subject to a demand that will be shaped mainly by utilitarian concerns of which desirable jobs are available in what quantity? If we do so, we may end by rationalizing schooling in an econometric sense but loosing, in the bargain, all that makes us human — and perhaps ultimately the very earth which gives us life.

The Instruments of Privatization

Aside from direct grants to private schools, two classic instruments for encouraging private schools at public expense have appeared and reappeared in various guises over the years. The first is a voucher system in which all or some students attending private schools bring government tuition subsidies with them. The Assisted Places Scheme in England is a limited-scope voucher plan within this broad definition. The second instrument is some form of tax-credit in which parents who send their children to private schools receive a credit on their income tax related in some way to the amount they spent on private schools up to some maximum allowable amount. California has recently attempted to establish such an educational tax-credit system.[37] Advocates of each instrument argue eloquently and intricately that their preferred instrument is the best means of fostering private education and thereby increasing and diffusing educational choice.

Vouchers

Quite simply an educational voucher functions as a sort of education coupon redeemable for educational services at a private (or sometimes a public) school. Like food coupons or stamps, the bearer is entitled to use the voucher to pay all or part of the tuition charged by a school. A voucher does not have to be a physical coupon, of course; it can be simply a per-pupil amount that government agrees to pay in respect of eligible pupils enrolled in a fee-charging school.

Among the advantages claimed by voucher advocates for such an instrument are the following:

1   Vouchers are not direct aid to a school. They are directed to schools by parental choice.
2   Unlike tax-credits, vouchers provide equal benefits to all, low-income families and high-income families alike. In particular, unless accompanied by a means test, they are unaffected by other elements in the taxation maze.
3   Only parents with children in school benefit from voucher schemes whereas some tax-credit schemes provide benefits to other benefactors of fee-charging schools (e.g., sponsoring grandparents or friends).
4   The possibility of unethical collusion to exploit the maximum value of available tax-credits to the detriment of state revenues is avoided.
5   Vouchers can be used for educational expenses and nothing else.
6   Vouchers require no more or less government regulation than tax-credits and are therefore preferable given their other advantages.[38]

The principal advantage claimed for the voucher is its universality, its ability to treat people who are very different for tax purposes on an equal footing. Vouchers are not, supporters suggest, direct aid to schools. They simulate and realize many of the advantages of free-market choice because parents decide which school(s) their children will attend. The user-benefit nature of the private education subsidy is clear and unmistakable in a voucher system which precludes benefits to other benefactors who could, as was attempted in California, easily be 'written into' tax-credit schemes. In short, vouchers avoid the manipulation of tax-credit benefits for maximum personal advantage. Finally, unless the principle of accountability for funds appropriated is completely abandoned,[39] some form of school approval process will be required under any aid program and the voucher method is no worse than any other in this administrative and control requirement.

Tax Credits

Advocates of tax credits, on the other hand, regard them as superior, because:

1 Complete parental choice is maintained in directing funds toward fee-charging schools.
2 A mechanism as effective as that of the voucher is provided whereby only expenses up to a certain ceiling are reimbursed by the government.
3 Tax-credits can be tailored to integrate in a planned and purposeful manner with other tax measures. Any desired degree of progressivity (or regressivity) can be built into them.
4 The support of persons other than parents toward the costs of education in fee-charging schools can be encouraged and that is to everyone's benefit.
5 Ancillary expenses necessary to education but not directly reflected in tuition fees can be recognized.
6 The same regulatory procedure for determining school eligibility for benefit claims would be required as under any other aid plan and therefore tax-credits are superior given their other advantages.

The crux of the tax-credit case is the ease with which it can be tailored to take into consideration relevant personal income and other tax structure considerations. Treating people equally who are unequal in their ability to pay is unfair, the tax-credit argument goes. Borrowing an argument from public finance that unequals should be treated unequally,[40] tax-credit advocates hold that giving high-income parents the same benefit as low-income parents does little to enlarge the choice of those who have the least choice under exclusively public-sector arrangements. The rich can easily augment a voucher and provide even more expensive schooling than they might otherwise have selected for their children, while the poor may find their voucher of the same value insufficient to offer them any practical choice at all. Furthermore, no defensible reason exists, in any public funding process, to deny particular benefits of schooling to *any* who contribute to paying its costs. Given their advantages, and the fact that tax-credits require no more or less regulation and control than other forms of aid, they are superior to vouchers.

Conclusion

In opening the Pandora's box of issues and arguments, which is the stuff of this chapter, I shared my perception that neither side in the debate, neither the advocates of privatization nor the champions of monolithic public education, had the makings of a knock-out blow in their arsenal of arguments. Both sides, however, raise issues and proffer arguments which command increasing attention not only among educators, policy-makers and politicians, but among parents, the business community and those who represent our religions, cultures and systems of belief.

Although a decisive victory of privatizers is unlikely in any major schooling arena, neither is movement toward creation or recreation of monopolistic state operated educational giants — not even at the primary and secondary levels. The future would appear to be one in which the values of publicly operated and privately operated schools, institutes and universities are continually, carefully and repeatedly weighed against one another, sifted and winnowed in ever more complex and far-reaching fields of argumentation. At best this can lead to cooperation and mutual respect between private and public-sector educators, a friendly but dynamic and determined competition in which each recognizes and respects the probable excesses which lay beyond a total victory for one or the other sector. An ongoing and vigorous debate about public and private sector education conducted in a spirit of compromise, a debate which puts the common good at the fore, can become a nexus of social policy-making which draws out the best of free-market choice and universalist provision. At worst, this debate can lead to confrontation and paralysis. In any case, the debate will not go away and it will not end in a decisive victory for one or the other agenda of social purpose.

Over all of the recent societal, technological and contextual changes within which schooling occurs, there looms the inescapable fact that, as nations and peoples, we are not who we once were. Our global village has witnessed mass migrations in recent years which dwarf the celebrated migrations of the past. In not a few countries and regions, the historical majority find themselves close to becoming a minority in their own land. The burgeoning multicultural reality of many rich nations, and even of some poor nations, demands close attention to the arguments underpinning what may have become the most politically potent claim and counterclaim of all concerning schooling arrangements.

Notes

1 The only exception would be Holland, but I do not regard Dutch schools as authentic examples of private provision (see p. 82).
2 Heyneman has developed this idea in several places. Recently he did so in a presentation to the American Education Finance Association Annual Meeting, see Stephen P. Heneman, 'A look at the 1990s: Financing education a decade from now in developing countries' (Paper delivered at the Annual Meeting of the American Education Finance Association, Tampa, Florida, 18 March 1988), p. 17.
3 See Figure 4.3, p. 54).
4 See pp. 17–18.
5 Patricia Lines, 'The new private schools and their historic purpose', *Phi Delta Kappan*, 67 (January 1986), p. 378.
6 See, for instance, Jean Barman, *Growing up British in British Columbia: Boys in Private School* (Vancouver: University of British Columbia Press, 1984), p. 79; and Peter Cookson, Jr., 'Boarding schools and the moral community', *The Journal of Educational Thought*, 16 (August 1982), pp. 89–97.
7 Penny Moss, 'A response to Mel Shipman', *Orbit*, 16 (April 1985), p. 14.
8 Henry Giroux, *Ideology, Culture and the Process of Schooling* (Philadelphia: Temple University Press and Falmer Press Ltd., 1981), pp. 75–112.
9 Peter Brimelow, 'Public and private schools: The need for competition', *Education Digest*, 49 (April 1984), p. 15.
10 See p. 10.
11 Peter Brimelow, 'Public and private schools: The need for competition', *op cit.*, p. 17.
12 Brimelow advocates vouchers as a form of public support for private education. In his view, vouchers are the means to deliver public edu-

cation from its status as 'a curious and anomalous experiment with socialism'. See Brimelow, 'Public and private schools: The need for competition', *op cit.*, p. 17.

13   Brimelow, 'Public and private schools: The need for competition', *op cit.*, p. 17.

14   The most recent example is the critique of the efforts of Coleman, Hoffer and Kilgore's effort to compare the quality of education offered in American public and private schools. See Kern Alexander and Aaron Pallas, 'Private schools and public policy: New evidence on cognitive achievement in public and private schools', *Sociology of Education*, 56 (October 1983), pp. 170–82; Kern Alexander and Aaron Pallas, 'In defense of "Private schools and public policy": Reply to Kilgore', *Sociology of Education*, 57 (January 1984), pp. 56–8; and Glen Cain and Arthur Goldberger, 'Public and private schools revisited', *Sociology of Education*, 56 (October 1983), pp. 208–18.

15   Increasingly exit to private schools is not a prerogative exercised only by the middle class and the rich. With increasing statistical frequency inner-city working poor are spending up to 10 per cent of their annual family income to give their children a chance they believe they can never have in inner-city public schools. See Virgil Blum, 'Why inner-city families send their children to private schools: An empirical study', in *Private Schools and the Public Good: Policy Alternatives for the Eighties*, ed. Edward M. Gaffney (Notre Dame: University of Notre Dame Press, 1981), pp. 17–24.

16   William Burt, 'The new campaign for tax credits: "Parochiaid" misses the point', in *Family Choice in Schooling*, ed. Michael Manly-Casimir (Toronto: D.C. Heath and Company, 1981), p. 157.

17   See, for example, Blum, 'Why inner-city families send their children to private schools: an empirical study', *op cit.*, pp. 17–24.

18   Despite the difficulty of coping with rising teacher salary costs, the Catholic parochial schools have apparently recovered from the arrest in growth they experienced over the last decade. In fact, both Catholic and non-Catholic schools seem to be growing impressively in the United States at present. For details see Bruce Cooper, Donald McLaughlin and Bruno Manno, 'The latest word on private school growth', *Teachers College Record*, 85 (Fall 1983), pp. 88–98.

19   Richard Pring, 'Privatization in education', *Journal of Education Policy*, 2 (December 1987), p. 299.

20   Denis Doyle, 'A din of inequity: Private schools reconsidered', *Teachers College Record*, 82 (Summer 1981), p. 670.

21   William Burt, 'The new campaign for tax credits: "Parochiaid" misses the point', *op cit.*, p. 154.

22   Beginning with Pierre Bourdieu and Jean-Claude Passeron *Reproduction In Education, Society and Culture*, trans. Richard Nice (London: Sage Publications, 1977); and the celebrated *Equality of Educational Opportunity*

(Washington: U.S. Department of Health, Education and Welfare, 1966) documenting the study of Coleman *et al.*, in the US, researchers in various countries have conducted studies which show that, generically, public schools have little impact on educational or life chances. Individual teachers may indeed affect learning outcomes and life chances (as the teacher-effectiveness research literature suggests), but, until recently, major studies of schooling effects were not designed to examine teacher effects, only school-level effects.

23 John Bergen, 'Choice in schooling', *Journal of Educational Administration and Foundations*, 1 (June 1986), p. 40.

24 See p. 82.

25 Carolyn Gossage, *A Question of Privilege: Canada's Independent Schools* (Toronto: Peter Martin Associates, 1977), p. 280.

26 Phoebe Hall *et al.*, *Change, Choice, and Conflict in Social Policy* (London: Heinemann, 1975), pp. 475–86.

27 John Bergen, 'Choice in schooling', *op cit.*, pp. 46–7.

28 For a full discussion of Section II, paragraph 26 of the Universal Declaration, as it applies to a parental right to choose private schools, see E.L. Edmonds, 'In defense of the private schools', *Education Canada*, 21 (Fall 1981), pp. 21–3; and Jean Gagnon, 'Pour rendre l'éxcellence accessible', *Prospectives: Revue D'information et de Recherche en Éducation*, 22 (février 1986), p. 23.

29 As noted earlier (see p. 84), the Australian constitution has a clause of almost identical wording, but, in the Australian case, the courts have allowed a much less restrictive reading within which public funding of religious schools does not constitute an excessive entanglement.

30 See, for instance, Patricia Anthony, 'Public monies for private schools: The Supreme Court's changing approach', *Journal of Education Finance*, 12 (Spring 1987), pp. 592–605; and Denis Doyle, 'Public funding and private schooling: The state of descriptive and analytic research', in *Private Schools and the Public Good: Policy Alternatives for the Eighties*, ed. Edward Gaffney (Notre Dame: University of Notre Dame Press, 1981), pp. 71–8.

31 Mel Shipman, 'Funding independent schools', *Orbit*, 16 (February 1985), p. 9.

32 See William Garner and Jane Hannaway, 'Private schools: The client connection', in *Family Choice in Schooling*, ed. Michael Manly-Casimir (Toronto: D.C. Heath and Company, 1982), p. 127.

33 Geoffrey Walford, 'How dependent is the independent sector?' *Oxford Review of Education*, 13 (September 1987), p. 278.

34 Basil Bernstein, *Class, Codes and Control* (London: Routledge and Kegan Paul, 1971), vol. 1, pp. 170–87.

35 Charles Perrow, *Complex Organizations: A Critical Essay*, 3rd. ed. (New York: Random House, 1986), p. 270.

36 Chester E. Finn, Jr., 'Why public and private schools matter', *Harvard Educational Review*, 51 (November 1981), p. 513.

37 John Coons and Stephen Sugarman, 'Educational tax credits versus school vouchers: Comment on the California tuition tax credit proposal', in *Family Choice in Schooling*, ed. Michael Manly-Casimir (Toronto: D.C. Heath and Company, 1981), pp. 169–77.

38 *Ibid.*

39 See discussion on p. 133.

40 See note 9, Chapter 2.

Chapter 8

The Pluralist Agenda and Education

Case 10

Claim

To be just to all its members and provide more equal educational opportunity and life chances, authentically multicultural education is required, that is, education for minority persons at least partially in their language and of their culture. Such education does not merely seek to create good feelings toward minority cultures and languages, it actively seeks to preserve and develop them. Publicly operated schools cannot escape their mainstream culture bias and assimilationist past, and so the task of educating minorities is best left to uniquely minority schools.

The way to peace and social harmony is through cohesive diversity, not through assimilation and enforced sameness in culture, language and belief. Social melting pots do not work, especially in the midst of the rapid demographic changes occurring in many technologically advanced nations. Schools, therefore, should be organized along lines of language, culture, belief and ethical commitment. Public schools cannot escape the pervasive homogenization which results from their mandate to be all things to all persons, although determining just what that mandate may entail is becoming more and more difficult as we become ever more differentiated culturally. In fact, the public schools with their melting-pot mandate and ethos may be more in-strumental than anything else in producing nations of people afraid to commit themselves to *any* values at all, perhaps even people unsure that values have any meaning in human existence. This closing of the mind to moral reality and to the larger questions of human existence has come about precisely because of the moral dessication of education committed to everyone's values and hence to no one's.[1] In any case, given their mandate to be all things to all persons, publicly operated schools are unlikely candidates for the operation of programs differentiated along cultural, linguistic, moral and religious lines.

Counterclaim

> *Despite a lot of bad press, assimilation works, and it works to the benefit of both minority persons and their host societies. Public schools should be given both tools and a renewed mandate to pursue effectively their historical task of integrating minorities into the cultural, social, economic and linguistic fabric of their host societies in an efficient and humane way.*

In the end, all must live and work in more or less unitary national societies. Schooling which fails to provide minority children with full competence in the dominant language and culture of their nation or region fails to equip minority students for life and work in their host societies. Adequate differentiation along cultural and linguistic lines can be provided by creating alternative schools in the public-sector, schools that at the same time, however, ensure a common core of necessary basic skills, knowledge and values shared by all students. Foremost among those shared values should be tolerance of diversity.

The Ultimate Goal: What Kind of Society?

Consciously or unconsciously, our ideas about public policy are shaped by our vision of the kind of society we would like to live in. This is especially true in the culturally symbolic and formative realm of education. The bottom-line social policy question is whether we want societies divided along cultural, linguistic, religious and moral commitment lines, cultural mosaics, or whether we want to use social, and especially educational, policy as a melting pot to homogenize societal values, mores and language to the greatest extent possible consistent with a reasonable degree of individual creativity and identity.

The shortest distance between two points in public policy, however, is rarely, if ever, a straight line. Much evidence exists today that assimilationist social and educational policies have failed massively for certain minorities and have left them far worse off both

151

individually and collectively than they might have been if had they not been forced through education programs which simply submerged them in the language and culture of their host societies. In short, assimilationist policies sold as a means to raise and equalize the life chances of minorities by giving them 'the same educational opportunities as everyone else', have often left them ghettoized in ethnic enclaves of ostracism and despair.

What has gone wrong, however, is not so much that people of similar cultural backgrounds live together in certain areas, but that their cultures, languages and beliefs have been systematically excluded from the schools, in fact defined by the schools as something other than 'education'. Within the ethnocentric vision of an educated person legitimated by the schools, persons who exhibited non-mainstream cultural characteristics were by definition 'uneducated' — and thus undesirable for higher status and income jobs.

Two realizations have helped change the policies of governments toward minority languages and cultures in the schools. First, assimilationist policies have failed, indisputably and massively, for minority groups determined to maintain a group identity, or at least unwilling or unable to blend into the cultural fabric of their host societies. Either unwilling or unable (or both) to turn their backs on their ethnic identity, groups such as the migrant workers in Europe and aboriginal peoples throughout the world have quite simply failed to adopt the culture and education of their host societies. Confronted with the massive and evident failure of assimilationist education policies to assimilate such minorities, governments and policy-makers are increasingly facing the painful dilemma of either sending good money after bad by continuing to sanction and underwrite such exercises in futility or changing the mandate of strategic educational policy as it touches minority persons.

In any case, cultural and linguistic homogeneity as a primary goal of social policy seems in trouble everywhere. Even minorities whose members have acquired sufficient knowledge and skill in the cultural norms and language of their host societies to enjoy a socioeconomic distribution similar to, or even better than, the rest of society, are increasingly seeking to retain their own particular linguistic and cultural heritage. The last decade has seen a renaissance of cultural awareness and expression for many peoples in many lands. In Canada, for instance, the prolonged, determined and eventually successful efforts of Ukrainians in Alberta to obtain government funding for schools offering up to half their instruction in Ukrainian has set a new Canadian benchmark for the role of minority languages and cultures in the schooling of minority children. What is especially interesting about the Ukrainian case is that Ukrainians have been very successful generally in Western Canada and so this is one indisputable case among many of members of an ethnic group wishing to preserve their cultural and linguistic heritage *for its own sake.*

The increasing proportion of national populations accounted for by ethnic minorities (visible and invisible) is helping even timorous or tradition-bound politicians in many countries to see pluralist ideas of social purpose in a steadily more favourable light. The simple, politically crucial fact confronting business and governments in most technologically advanced countries is that minorities wield increasing clout in the marketplace and at the ballot box. With declining birthrates that are already below the replacement rate in most such countries, and with heavy immigration of culturally disparate groups to maintain existing population bases, being seen as an ardent assimilationist can be both financially and politically ruinous.

Given this demographic ascendancy of minorities — indeed, in some cases their immediate threat to outnumber collectively the members of their host societies — the dictums of the pluralist social purpose agenda[2] are now actively discussed in national and regional political fora. Partisans of both the conservative and equalitarian agendas have come to see increasing value in preserving and developing minority languages and cultures, indeed, of weaving them into the fabric of new national identities. The major question which divides conservative from equalitarian ideologues is the question of whether this pluralism should be purely cultural or whether it should also be structural, that is, whether different institutions should exist for different groups in society. In educational policy, this comes down to the question of who should control education differentiated along culture and language lines — and to the closely related one of how differentiated such education should be. In general, champions of free-market education align themselves with more control by minorities themselves and less by government, ultimately even with private, ethnic schools.[3] At the other pole are equalitarians who believe that adequate differentiation along cultural and language lines can be provided by publicly operated alternative programs and schools.

The turnaround in opinion regarding the claims of the pluralist social purpose agenda, however, is by no means unanimous. Backlash is inevitable wherever the cultural hegemony of a dominant group is threatened. A clearly dominant language and culture confer economic and political hegemony on those who live in that language and who reflect the habits, behaviours, lifestyle and values of that culture. Loss of linguistic and cultural dominance is loss of jobs, prestige and power.

Each country confronted with dilution of its traditional linguistic and cultural majority (or majorities) develops 'right-wing' political factions or fringe groups seeking to restore and secure the universal dominance of its language and culture. Ironically, such groups are drawn by the logic of their purpose into the equalitarian social purpose camp. All members of society, they emphasize, need to be competent in the national language(s). Therefore, they conclude, all children should be educated in the principal language and within the dominant culture of their country or region. No idea of balkanization and free choice here. All should be educated in the same way in schools that offer a common curriculum firmly and unequivocally rooted in the language and culture of the traditionally dominant group.

Beyond the emotional political contest for linguistic and cultural status and power, what is the history of minority education policy and what are the competing arguments, beliefs and assumptions which shape that increasingly important sub-arena of schooling? For answers to these questions, questions which have figured large in my research and writing activities over the last several years, I have been driven to the work of Stacy Churchill, most particularly, although by no means exclusively, to his summary and analysis of a recent Organization for Economic Cooperation and Development (OECD) study of minority education policy in OECD countries.[4] In that report, Churchill provides a powerful framework for understanding the history and current state of educational policy-making affecting minority groups. The understanding offered by this framework, and by close scrutiny of the assumptions which underpin it,[5] go far toward organizing and evaluating the claims of the pluralist social purpose agenda on educational policy-making and on the shape of schooling in the most general terms.

Minority Education: Key Assumptions and Propositions

Minorities are never unaffected by immersion in an alien culture and language. At the very least, minority persons must generally obtain a veneer of minimal proficiency in the dominant language and of acceptability within the dominant culture in order to survive economically. At best, they become bilingual and bicultural (with all the ambiguities implied by these terms).[6] Typically, even where the ancestral language is not rapidly eroded — and rapid erosion is the outcome for most minorities — their home use of that language, and their lived culture at home and within their 'ethnic' community (in the broadest sense), is heavily influenced by the surrounding mainstream culture. Mass media, particularly television, ensures that the home of virtually every minority person is continually bombarded with the language and culture of the host society so that the option of maintaining the home or ethnic neighbourhood as a secure cultural enclave is simply no longer available.

The erosion and mutation of language — and equally of culture — pose, moreover, a very difficult decision for those who seek to create learning environments to preserve and foster an ancestral language and culture. What language — and especially what culture — should be preserved, the traditional one or the current one? These can be very different. A people with a tradition of fierce independence and self-reliance, for instance, can become a people with a strong 'welfare mentality' if they spend a long enough time near the bottom rung of the socioeconomic ladder. Deciding what is 'authentic' for a given minority in a given context is always one of the most difficult, painful and pervasive problems of giving shape to heritage language and culture programs.

Erosion and mutation create a spectrum of language and cultural loss ranging from minimal to complete. Some minorities lose more or less completely their traditional language and culture while others retain much intact. Three questions arise. First, what kinds of policy rationales have been and can be applied to those who still retain the active use of their language and a culture similar in many respects to the culture of their ancestors? Second, what policy rationales have been and can be applied to those whose ancestral language and cultures are lost? Finally, are the rationales different and do they lead to different policy problems and solutions?

What policy-makers see as a problem is inevitably grounded in their vision of what society ought to be and become, on their own particular view of the nature of the public good. The solutions they propose to the problems they perceive depend in turn on their assumptions about how various policies affect what people can and will do. Research can shed light on the effects of existing policies, although it can never demonstrate unequivocally to what degree any particular effect is the result of any particular policy or combination of policies. Where radically new policy solutions are being considered, however, only assumptions and beliefs can fill the void left by inexperience with the new arrangements. For this reason, as much as for any other, governments have long had a strong preference for small changes and incremental policy-making.[7] In the end, new approaches to minority education policy stem mainly from changes in belief, not from empirical evidence, although inferences from empirical evidence may influence changes in belief.

What, then, are the generic ways of making sense of the poor school performance of certain minority groups? What kinds of solutions based upon what kinds of assumptions do these different policy problem statements produce? Finally, how do these problems and solutions apply to those struggling to maintain a living culture and language on the one hand, and to those who have already lost their ancestral culture and language on the other? The answers to all these questions exist, most explicitly, some latently, in the Churchill framework.[8]

The Churchill Framework

Churchill concludes that OECD countries exhibit six different stages of belief about the principal problem and preferred solution to poor educational performance and participation on the part of certain minorities, see table 8.1. Moreover, he presents compelling evidence of a stagewise progression up this ladder of belief from stage-1 assimilationism toward stage-6 language equality. Certainly that progression has been fitful and irregular, but the overall trend is not in doubt. On the whole, assimilationist policies are giving way to less ethnocentric views of educational purpose. Despite the common curriculum thrust of the current round of educational reform, more, not less, room is being provided in the educational policy frameworks of OECD countries for minority languages and cultures.

All OECD countries began with stage-1 policies toward minorities, that is, with a classic assimilationist view of the educational problems certain minorities experience in the schools and of what to do about them. Stage 1 is the simplest, and most time-honoured, form of victim blaming. Within a stage-1 perspective, the problem of poor minority performance in school lies within the students themselves. Such students have a learning deficit in the majority language, and in traditional school subjects, which manifests itself in much the same way as mental retardation or a learning disability. Minority students don't do well in school because they lack facility in academic registers of the majority language. The solution, within a stage-1

Table 8.1 Stages in state policies toward the education of minorities

Model	Perceived Problem	Policy Response
Stage 1: Learning deficit	Lack of competence in majority language results in problems similar to retardation or learning disability.	More intensive instruction in majority language. Remedial approach to language.
Stage 2: Socially-linked learning deficit	Language deficit. Same as for Stage 1 except that problems in family's social status are considered causes of poor achievement.	Same as for Stage 1 but special measures to help minority students adjust to majority society.
Stage 3: Learning deficit from cultural/social differences	Language deficit: as in first two stages. But greater emphasis on consequences of cultural differences on students' self-concept. Partial responsibility placed on society and schools for not accepting and responding to minority culture.	Same as for first two stages but with 'multi cultural' teaching programs designed to teach all students about minority culture.
Stage 4: Learning deficit from deprivation of mother tongue	Language deficit as in first three stages but a major cause of poor achievement is assumed to be premature loss of mother tongue. This loss assumed to inhibit learning in majority language. Social problems and differences also blamed as in Stage 2.	Same remedial approaches to teaching of majority language. Support provided out of school hours for home study of minority language as a subject and occasionally as a medium of instruction.
Stage 5: Private use language maintenance	Minority language of group threatened by disappearance if not supported by government. Minority disadvantaged in education by weaker social position of language and culture. Minority has long-term rights to survival, but expected to enter majority society outside school.	Minority language used as medium of instruction, usually as exclusive medium in earlier years. Majority language required subject of study at least from late elementary years. Transition to majority language usually required for highest levels of educational system.
Stage 6: Language equality	Languages of minority and majority assumed to have equal rights in society. Language of smaller groups requires special support to ensure broad social use: education viewed as only one field of language policy application.	Minority language granted status of official language, separate educational institutions, usually under administration by relevant language group. Support measures extend beyond educational systems to all phases of official business, sometimes to private sector as well.

Source: Churchill, 1986, pp. 54–6.

view, is more intensive instruction in the majority language and a remedial approach to all aspects of language learning; in short, more of the same but in stronger doses. Equality of educational opportunity, in such a view, consists in sameness of program. To have an equal opportunity, minority students should get the same curriculum taught in the same way as other students (although perhaps with some extra help).

The next stage evident in the evolution of the thought of OECD policy-makers regarding minority failure in the schools (socially-linked learning deficit problem) involves blaming the victims as a group. In this view, the problem with minority students becomes the backwardness and ignorance of the social reference group from which they spring. Language and learning deficits are not really the fault of lazy, obstinate or stupid students but of the poor social (and usually economic) status of their families. The solution, however, in such a problem formulation is much the same as at stage 1, more remediation of one sort or another, with the addition that the assimilationist intent of stage 2 is often dramatized for minority students in the particularly vivid and unmistakable form of 'welcoming' classes specifically aimed at the fastest possible linguistic and cultural replacement.

Stage 3 policy-makers formulate the problem of poor minority performance as a learning deficit which arises from social and cultural differences but acknowledge that the majority society and its schools may be partly responsible for the poor self-concept and low motivation among poorly performing minority students. In short, both the larger society and its schools share a bit of the blame with the student, his family and his social reference group.[9] Again the preferred solution is intensive remediation but coupled with 'multicultural' programs aimed at making all students more knowledgable about and open to each other's cultures. Typically, as well, stage-3 soul-searching about societal and school complicity in minority school failure leads to efforts to purge schools of materials and teaching which present negative stereotypes of minority persons.

Stage 4 is a watershed in the evolution of belief about what goes wrong in minority education. In stage 4, the school failure of minorities is attributed to mother-tongue deprivation. Children cannot be expected, the stage-4 argument goes, to absorb conceptually complex material through the medium of a language they only partially understand. The effects of this 'submersion' in a majoritarian curriculum taught in the majority language is particularly devastating and alienating for very young children. Loss of mother tongue adversely affects the educational future and life chances of such children and should be deliberately slowed. Put otherwise, educational policy and the schools should do what they can to create *out-of-school* programs for the 'home' study of minority languages as a subject (the type of program frequently referred to as 'heritage' language programs in some parts of Canada) or perhaps even as a medium of instruction. The fundamental difference between a stage-4 idea of the problem of minority education and lower-stage ideas is that, at stage 4, the minority language and culture itself becomes part of the solution, not just part of the problem. While the minority language is considered useful here mainly as a transitional device, rapid loss of maternal language is definitely seen as part of the problem. The ethnocentrism of stage 4, however, is only marginally less than that of earlier stages. The minority language, after all, is not allowed into the fabric of formal, compulsory education and its main educational purpose is, in fact, to hasten its own demise.

Stage 5 accepts the intrinsic worth of minority languages, their inherent right to exist and develop. In a stage-5 view, minorities have a right as *a group* to survive, maintain and develop their ancestral languages, and nurture a distinctive identity. Moreover, government has an obligation to help minorities accomplish this when they are disadvantaged in education by the weak social position of their languages and cultures. Out of such a belief system grow educational programs which use minority languages as a medium of instruction, in-school programs which spring, to a significant degree, from the ancestral languages and cultures of minority students. Nonetheless, within stage 5, a normative expectation exists that higher education will be available only in the majority language and that *all* educational programs must therefore provide a solid foundation in the majority language.

Stage 6 is the consummate realization of cultural relativism, complete statutory language equality. Stage 6 has only rarely been approached as official policy and is perhaps only conceivable where society is not fragmented into too many culturally and linguistically disparate groups. In a stage-6 view, all languages are equal and minorities have a right to live and to administer their affairs in their own language and within their own cultural milieu. In stage-6 policy logic, no expectation exists that business, higher education or anything else should be in one language rather than another for the whole nation-state. Stage 6 is the minority education problem viewed through the eyes of the committed structural pluralist.

In reality, any of these problem concepts and solutions can be applied to those who no longer speak their ancestral language as well as to those who seek to retain a language still alive but endangered, but the reasons for and difficulties with doing so differ considerably when the problem is language restoration rather than preservation.[10] Language restoration is clearly a much more problematic undertaking than retaining a language still widely understood and used by members of a minority group. One cannot, furthermore, except in an indirect sense, argue that maternal language loss is an important cause of poor educational performance and school persistence on the part of a minority that has lost its language and culture. The options in the case of language loss are either some form of compensatory majority language education (e.g., second dialect programs, remedial language programs or language stimulation), all clearly within the ambit of Churchill's stages 1 through 3, or, alternately, some degree of language restoration. Depending on the intensiveness of efforts at restoration and their success, they could be seen as part of any of a stage 4 through 6 approach. If the intent were merely to bolster self-image by providing a minimal and short-lived contact with the ancestral language, a stage-4 rationale would predominate. If functional fluency and actual use in the community were the objective, a stage-5 view of the problem would be at stake. If official use of the language for government and commerce were the objective (as in, perhaps, the restoration of Hebrew in post-war Israel), a stage-6 rationale would apply to that language. The principal reason for attempting some degree of language restoration would certainly be a conviction that only such a step would sufficiently reverse the alienation from formal education of minority groups whose culture and language the schools have too long repressed and denigrated. Only incorporating that language and culture into a school sanctioned vision of the 'educated person', advocates of language restoration argue, can reverse that alienation from learning and schooling.

Language and Culture Balance: Beliefs and Assumptions

Whatever the current condition of the ancestral languages and cultures of given minority groups, the advisability of vernacular language programs turns ultimately on beliefs about three matters:

1 The type of society desired, especially the desirability of promoting or restraining cultural and linguistic diversity.
2 What should constitute a minimum core curriculum for *all* students of all backgrounds.

3   The relationship between overall learning and the percentage
    of the total curriculum drawn from the minority language and
    culture.

All these beliefs are interrelated, even in a certain sense, interlocked.
The first two beliefs are set by one's overall concept of social purpose,
in particular, the degree to which cultural and, by implication,
structural pluralism are seen as serving the public good. The third
belief concerns a desirable balancing of minority and mainstream
curriculum content and language usage, and depends on which of
Churchill's stages one uses to make sense of the poor school performance of certain minorities. Stage-1 beliefs, for instance, imply an idea
very different from stage-5 beliefs of how increasing the proportion
(however one chooses to quantify it) of the curriculum consecrated to
the minority language and culture affects overall learning in mainstream language and mainstream curriculum content. How much of
the curriculum one gives over to a minority language and culture
obviously sets limits to the amount of core curriculum shared by all
students and visa versa.

Culture is inevitably bound up in language — and one's sense of
self with both culture and language. To surrender one's language and
culture is to become someone else, collectively to become a different
people. Few individuals or peoples assimilate willingly into host
societies, although most probably wish to integrate into them. In
recent years, an emergent multicultural ethos has challenged the
fundamental assumptions of melting-pot social ideology, and even
those who assimilated quite willingly in the past are frequently
searching for their roots and identity in ancestral languages and
cultures. The school, as primary institutional symbol of culture — a
symbol, moreover, which appears to shape powerfully the language
use, culture and values of the young who are socialized there — is at
the heart of a never-ending struggle for control of what children learn,
how they speak and what they believe about themselves and the
world. Schools are indeed, 'arenas in which the deepest conflicts
within the societies they are meant both to reproduce and change are
played out'.[11] The most common ensigns in this battle are 'core
instruction' on the one hand, and, on the other, education rooted in
the assumptions, world view and habits of a minority, in a word,
'heritage education'.

The belief systems encompassed by Churchill's stages of minority
education policy spring from three different assumptions about
the impact on educational persistence and performance of weaving

minority languages and cultures into the fabric of educational programs. Do minority students stay in school longer, achieve better overall educational results, and realize greater personal and career success, however defined, if part or much of their education is in their maternal or ancestral language and derives important elements of its shape and content from their maternal culture? Or does heritage education adversely affect the educational performance of minority students?

Three answers are possible. Each assumes, in the first instance, that schools do 'make a difference' in some sense in the degree to which students remain in school, and in the educational achievement and life chances of students. This assumption, of course, may have been questioned by educational researchers from Jensen, Jencks and Coleman[12] until the recent wave of 'effective schools' research (with all of its flaws, omissions and blind spots).[13] Nonetheless, widespread universal compulsory attendance laws and the fact that most people who are able to do so willingly pay to support schools and send their children to them are powerful evidence of enduring faith in the principle that schools can *at least potentially* make a difference. This faith in some sort of schooling efficacy is a pivotal assumption in developing answers to the question of how minority heritage programs affect minority learning.

Each of us has some idea of what educational quality means. No two people are likely to agree completely on what indicators should be used and how they should be weighted, but that is unimportant for understanding three dominant beliefs about the educational effects of including minority languages and culture in the substance of what we define as 'education'. Imagine that some index exists which measures adequately what you consider to be the essential elements of educational quality (probably some combination of attendance and retention data with data on some mix of easy and hard-to-measure achievement objectives). The fact that everyone will have a different index is irrelevant to the important arguments here.

Given an index which represents quality in conventional, mainstream education as you understand it, imagine using this index to measure the performance (and persistence) of a large group of minority students of a particular ethnicity. This group is one with a particularly poor track record in traditional schools and programs. Three generic belief types are possible, regarding the educational effects of minority language instruction and cultural content. For those committed to the assimilationist assumptions of social and educational purpose underlying Churchill's first three stages of

Figure 8.1 *Assumptions of assimilationist policy about educational performance*

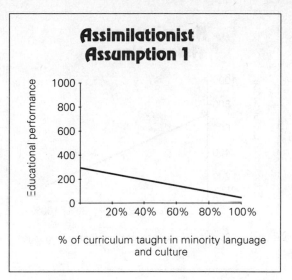

minority education policy thought, a clear and unavoidable trade-off appears to exist between mainstream and minority-based curriculum content. In simplest linear form, as more of the curriculum (time, resources, and so forth) is given over to minority content, less learning in mainstream curriculum domains occurs. More Chinese means less of the three rs. Within assimilationist ideas of the minority education policy problem, adding minority content reduces the performance of minority students on measures of mainstream educational achievement and attainment.

Consciously or unconsciously, assimilationists who believe that minorities are fated by their genes or social background, or by both, to poor educational performance, also believe in a relationship similar to that shown in figure 8.1. In this belief, for reasons over which schools have no control, the performance and retention of the minority is at best abysmal. Furthermore, they can only get worse as more of the mainstream curriculum is traded off against heritage culture 'frills'.

Alternatively, a committed but less fatalistic assimilationist might believe that better remedial programs could significantly raise the performance of 'educationally disadvantaged' minorities. Of course, the whole thrust of the OECD special population data was in the opposite direction, namely that more intensive efforts at remediation (whether labelled as remediation, language stimulation or special

Figure 8.2 *Assimilationist idealization of the performance/content relation*

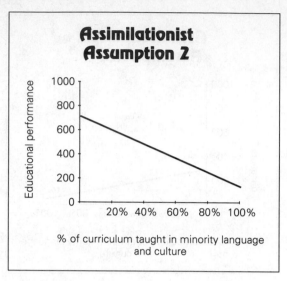

education) had little positive effect on school performance or retention for such minorities.[14] Nonetheless, the complete assimilationist fantasy, illustrated in figure 8.2, is still an article of faith for the most ardent defenders of a universal, comprehensive, common curriculum. In this view, the problem is one of under-resourced, ill-planned and mistargeted remediation rather than any inherent flaw in the assimilationist goals of eradicating and replacing the languages and cultures of minority students. In such a view, as in the genetic or social deficiency view shown in figure 8.1, more minority language and culture inevitably spells decline in retention and performance for minorities with poor track records in the schools. The difference is that adherents to this idealized assimilationist fantasy (the way things *should* turn out, but don't, according to traditional assimilationist ideas of the minority education problem) avoid attributing the school failure of such groups to genetics or to fatally flawed social reference groups by insisting that we simply haven't yet found and implemented 'appropriate' methods of remediation. If educators once get these right, such persons contend, school success and equal life chances will be just around the corner for minorities who traditionally fill out the lower end of school performance distribution curves. The bottom-line implication is that the solution to the problem of minorities with poor school performance is more experimentation with, and research into, various approaches to remediation — not incorporation of minority cultures and languages into the school program.

In any case, the more remediation that is added to the educational program of minority students the less time and resources are available for heritage education. A sort of discontinuity must, therefore, be imagined in the relationships depicted in Figures 8.1 and 8.2. Time and resources committed to remediation, after all, limit the amount of minority language and culture that can be included in a school program.

Either of these two assimilationist beliefs concerning the relation ship between mainstream curriculum performance and minority curriculum content can be, and frequently is, invoked as a reason for avoiding or slowing efforts at heritage education. Another important agenda, however, imposes itself on all discussions of the balance between mainstream and heritage education. Only the most politically naive miss the point that education, no less than government and public administration generally, is an exercise in cultural domination in which the bottom-line stakes are jobs, income level, prestige and power. One trade-off *is* certain, after all, in the heritage education debate. More pupil-hours of instruction in a minority language and culture means fewer person hours of employment and less income and policy-making power for mainstream educators. Thus equalitarians who choose to define equality of educational opportunity in assimilationist terms, and there is a natural affinity between the two beliefs, can be assured of considerable support from those who presently staff and run schools with programs taught in national language(s) and permeated by the culture and value assumptions of the national majority culture(s).

A third view exists, however, of the relationship between overall school performance and the proportion of the curriculum given over to minority language and culture. A contrary assumption about this relationship is that heritage education programs *improve* school retention and performance. In the case that minority language and culture content complements and enhances rather than obstructs learning mainstream curriculum in the dominant language, some version of the relationship shown in figure 8.3 must exist. In this view, more heritage education means better educational results rather than worse for traditionally poor performing minorities. In a belief system directly at odds with the principles of educational conservatism, but not aligned with the individualism of educational progressivism,[15] champions of this view insist that, up to some maximum, including minority content boosts all learning. Such a view is group and culture-centred (or at least group-focused), and thus generically different from the 'child-focused' education of older progressive thinkers in education.

Supporters of this view see minority content as complementing and supporting mainstream curriculum content. They believe the learning achievement of certain groups of minority students is low, in part at least, *because* of maternal language deprivation or *because* of the exclusion of their heritage from schools and from the school sanctioned definition of education.[16] Increasing the proportion of curriculum taught in a minority language and drawn from minority culture increases, at least up to some point of diminishing returns, performance in the mainstream curriculum. Some optimum level of performance (a transition from positive to negative slope in the diagram) must exist if one concedes the underlying assumption that schools effect, or at least affect, learning. The case that such a maximum must exist is quite simple. If *all* school instruction in programs for minority students occurred in their language and culture, they would only learn national language(s) and mainstream curriculum from the out-of-school environment. If schools have any positive effect at all, some instruction in the national languages and mainstream curriculum must be better than none. The assumption that heritage education complements mainstream education, however, demands that no heritage education should produce worse average results than some. Hence a maximum (or maxima) must exist in student performance between the extremes of no heritage education and no mainstream core curriculum.

The exact shape of the curve, however, is debatable and indeed no reason exists to assume that the curve would be the same in differ ent situations or at different times. What is important is the assumption that some degree of minority presence in the curriculum — and in that curriculum's implied definition of education — *supports* overall learning. How relatively high the maximum is seen to occur, and how far to the right along the minority content axis, depends on ideas about how strongly and up to what point minority content supports majoritarian learning. Since all of these relationships are ultimately matters of belief, it is unlikely that any two observers will agree about their particulars. This is especially true of figure 8.3, with its unfamiliar ring and controversial implications for those who teach in and administer mainstream culture schools.

Nonetheless, a fundamental conclusion of the OECD study of

Figure 8.3   Minority content supporting performance

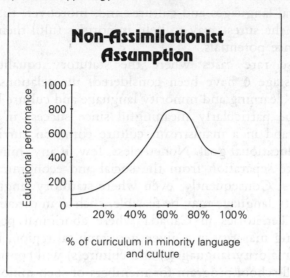

education for special populations is that minority education policy is moving steadily, if fitfully, toward problem definitions which assume that minority languages and cultures should become part of the fabric of the educational experience of minority persons and that their educational performance and attainment will improve as a result.[17] That is, governments are tiring of what they see as pouring good money after bad in an apparently futile search for the assimilationist holy grail: programs of remediation that really work for educationally disadvantaged groups. Instead, they look increasingly to in-school use of minority languages and cultures as means toward better educational performance for disadvantaged minorities.

As a first step, governments have come to favour policies aimed at using such minority languages as transitional devices to ease the task of learning the majority language and adjusting to the majority culture. In terms of Churchill's framework, most governments began nudging away from assimilationist approaches to minority education by sanctioning the use of minority languages in the lower primary grades in order to facilitate transition to mainstream language education. More recently, the same governments have begun moving toward policies of building a significant part of the educational program of minority students in their ancestral language and culture. The assumptions underlying such policies are those of Churchill's stage 5, namely that minorities have a right to maintain and develop their ancestral languages and cultures and, moreover, that honouring that right is the surest way to help minorities fulfil their educational and life-chance potentials.

In those rare cases where the statutory equality principles underlying stage 6 have been considered, the relationship between 'mainstream' learning and minority language and culture learning may no longer be particularly meaningful since success in the national language(s) and in a mainstream culture common curriculum is no longer an educational goal. Nonetheless, few, if any, minorities desire apartheid-like separation from the social and economic life of their host societies. Consequently, even where statutory language equality for a minority language may be feasible, such as in certain areas of the Northwest Territories in Canada where aboriginal people are the overwhelming majority in a given geographical region, it is virtually certain that majority language(s) and culture(s) will continue to figure in the overall school program for members of such minorities. In that sense, a figure 8.3 rationale may be quite appropriate to education aimed at language equality, so long as the objective is not the usually dubious one of unilingualism in the minority language.

A second major trend in minority education policy reported in the OECD study is a tendency for minorities to demand, be granted and assume more control over the education of their members. Churchill stops short of claiming a causal relation, but the evidence of the OECD study is clear that minority control tends to grow once minority language and culture become part of schooling. Part of the linkage is undoubtedly the universal but difficult issue of educational quality. Token minority language and culture programs may do more damage to than good for the image of self and people of minority persons. A badly thought out, poorly organized and under-resourced heritage education program reinforces the assimilationist message that the mainstream language and culture is what counts and all others are marginal — outside the substantive mandate of publicly funded schools. Hence the trend noted in the OECD study for concerns about quality to appear shortly after the introduction of heritage education programs. Furthermore, it is almost definitionally impossible for those who do not know a language and culture to plan and supervise high quality programs in them. As a result, the impetus toward quality in minority curriculum content has a logic about it which leads, however much the specifics of the process may vary, toward enhancing the control of minorities over the education of their young.

Conclusion

The OECD study contributes much toward understanding how the education of minorities is linked to ideas of social purpose. Through its framework of analysis, through its data on the historic development of minority-education policies across the Western world, and finally, through the assumptional analysis which it presents and implies, the study gives us a previously lacking policy gestalt for thinking about minorities and schooling. It reaffirms, moreover, that what we want our schools to do is inevitably shaped by what we think our national societies ought to become. Assimilationist policies, both in the educational arena and in the larger social policy arena grow from ethnocentricism. Ethnocentricism is difficult to maintain, however, in democratic political arenas where minorities can swing, or determine, the political balance of power. Nations awakened to an inescapably multicultural social, economic, political and linguistic reality within their borders become much more susceptible to the assumptions of the structural pluralist agenda of social purpose — and to parallel assumptions about educational purpose in Churchill's higher stage concepts of the minority education challenge. Perhaps, after all, we are most securely bound together where we are a community of communities. Our prospects for peace and prosperity may, as pluralists claim, be better if, while sharing much in culture, language and belief, we at the same time retain and take pride in our group identities. Such pluralist faith is the more palatable where assimilationism has been well tried and yet found wanting in its ability to secure a better life for minorities — as well as peace and security for the larger community.

What none of this argumentation touches directly is the second issue buried in the claim and counterclaim of case 10 presented at the beginning of this chapter, that is, the ability of publicly operated schools to embrace educational policies which diversify the substance of their educational programs along lines of language and culture. At the very least, a mandate to mount programs differentiated along such lines is a profound challenge to the political economy of public schooling. Jobs and careers are at stake as well as the most basic sense of educational mission. Where will lines be drawn? How finely? Who will decide where to draw them? How can the general public interest be combined with group specific interests in workable funding, governance and certification arrangements? Where language and religious lines cross rather than coincide (as in certain areas of Ontario and

Quebec with their matrices of Catholic and Protestant French and Catholic and Protestant English), how should they be sorted out?

The challenge of creating public schools differentiated along lines of language and culture is, in many ways, even greater than that of creating public schools differentiated along moral and religious lines. Many see 'hiving off' students from the common school along lines of ethnicity and language as a fundamental and intolerable affront to the view of public schooling which chartered it in the first place, a violation of the democratic social contract at state expense.[18] Yet others argue exactly the contrary, contending that only the state can properly monitor and regulate education, all the more so if local programs are to be substantively different from one another in language of instruction and cultural roots.

In short, the assumptional questions raised by the Churchill framework do not speak *directly* to the issue of private versus public operation, funding and regulation. Insofar, however, as they do suggest that everyone, and especially educationally disadvantaged groups, may benefit from educational programs more differentiated along lines of culture and language, they raise the spectre of some very heady practical and political challenges if the development of such alternatives is to occur directly under the public aegis. It also throws down the gauntlet before the assumptions and principles of traditional *educational* conservatism[19] and the neo-conservative 'core curriculum' movement. It equally challenges, however, the radical individualism of conventional educational progressivism.[20] Clearly any real-world resolution of these challenges will not be a matter of 'either-or'. Rather, they will be a balancing of what all should learn with what each should learn according to his own kind. Nonetheless, the most troubled waters in educational policy over the coming decades are unlikely to be the struggle of individualism versus universally mandated learning. They are far more likely to be the turbulence produced by the challenge of group identity rights in the ongoing ebb and flow of thinking about the advantages of private education as opposed to public education.

In any case, the lines of argumentation cross and cannot be disentangled with certainty. Nor can they be resolved with any finality. Debate will continue on many policy fronts in many lands about how far the balance of schooling should be tilted toward eclectic embrace of many languages and cultures and, at the same time, about how private or public the overall schooling arena should be in its operation, funding and regulation.

Notes

1   For a recent and insightful perspective on this aspect of the contemporary education and moral thought, see Allan Bloom, *The Closing of the American Mind* (New York: Simon and Schuster, 1987), perhaps most pointedly, the first two chapters.

2   See page 17.

3   In Alberta, for instance, which has provided generous public funding of private schools with few strings attached, 82 private schools distinguished by culture and language of instruction existed in 1984, see K. Leung, 'Ethnic schools and public education: A study of the relationship between ethnic schools and public education in Alberta' (Master's thesis, University of Calgary, 1984). For further information on the political evolution of private-school support in Alberta see Margaret Durnin, 'The New Alberta School Act', *Our Schools, Our Selves* 1 (October 1988), pp. 96–105.

4   Stacy Churchill, *The Education of Linguistic and Cultural Minorities in the OECD Countries* (Clevedon: Multilingual Matters Ltd., 1986).

5   For a more complete statement of my current thinking on the subject, refer to Jerry Paquette, 'Minority education policy: Assumptions and propositions', *Curriculum Inquiry* 19 (December 1989), pp. 405–20; and Jerry Paquette, 'From propositions to prescriptions: Belief, power and the problem of minority education', *Curriculum Inquiry* 19 (December 1989), pp. 437–51.

6   Where they must live and work with more than one national language in addition to their ancestral language, combining retention of their ancestral cultural and language with full participation in the larger economic and social life of their adopted land may require functional competence in three or more languages and cultures.

7   For a complete discussion of incrementalism in policy-making, see Ira Sharkansky, *The Routines of Politics* (New York: Van Nostrand-Reinhold, 1970).

8   For a compact summary, see Stacy Churchill, *The Education of Linguistic and Cultural Minorities in the OECD Countries, op cit.,* pp. 54–6.

9   For a full development of the concept of a social reference group, see Robert K. Merton *Social Theory and Social Structure* (1957; reprint, New York: The Free Press, 1965), pp. 225–386.

10 For a comprehensive review of some of the difficulties and dilemmas of language restoration efforts among American Indians, see Robert St. Clair and William Leap, eds, *Language Renewal among American Indian Tribes: Issues, Problems and Prospects* (Rosslyn, Virginia: National Clearinghouse for Bilingual Education, 1982).

11 Joseph Farrell, 'Cultural differences and curriculum inquiry', *Curriculum Inquiry* 17 (Spring 1987), pp. 1–7.

12   One could turn to Jensen for assurances that heredity is more important than schooling in determining school performance, as in Arthur Jensen, *Educability and Group Differences* (London: Methuen & Co. Ltd., 1973), especially pp. 243–53 and p. 259; or, in summary form, Arthur Jensen, 'Biogenetic perspectives: An introduction', in *Social Class, Race, and Psychological Development*, ed. Martin Deutsch, Irwin Katz and Arthur R. Jensen (New York: Holt, Rinehart and Winston, 1968), p. 9, where Jensen flatly states that '70 to 90 per cent of the variability in measured intelligence is attributable to genetic factors...'.

     Alternatively, Coleman offered initial (although subsequently much criticized) evidence, that environment — not schools — explained most variation in student achievement, see James S. Coleman *et al.*, *Equality of Educational Opportunity* (Washington: U.S. Department of Health, Education and Welfare, 1966), p. 22.

     For the view that neither 'family background, cognitive skill, educational attainment, nor occupational status explains men's [sic] incomes' (i.e., that schooling and a lot of other common explanations for variations in life chances are false), see Christopher Jencks, *Inequality: A Reassessment of the Effect of Family and Schooling in America* (Hammondsworth: Penguin, 1972), p. 226.

13   I have recently synthesized the common criticisms of 'effective schools' research in a paper on the meaning of quality in education, see Jerry Paquette, 'The quality conundrum: Assessing what we cannot agree on', in *Scrimping or Squandering?: Financing Canadian Schools*, ed. Stephen Lawton and Rouleen Wignall (Toronto: OISE Press, 1989), pp. 11–28. An excellent short critical review of the effective-schools literature is in Doris Ryan, *Developing a New Model of Teacher Effectiveness: Lessons Learned from the IEA Classroom Environment Study* (Toronto: Ministry of Education, 1986), pp. 1–14.

14   Churchill, *The Education of Linguistic and Cultural Minorities in the OECD Countries, op cit.*, especially pp. 114–48.

15   See discussion on the interplay of conservative and equalitarian social theory with conservative and progressive educational ideology on pages 68 through 71.

16   See p. 303.

17   Churchill, *The Education of Linguistic and Cultural Minorities in the OECD Countries, op cit.*, pp. 149–62.

18   Penny Moss, 'A Response to Mel Shipman', *Orbit* 16 (April 1985), p. 14.

19   See p. 71.

20   See p. 68.

Chapter 9

The Schooling Crucible: Education and Our Future

Schools are but one among many influences on social evolution — and on the physical, intellectual and moral development of children. Nonetheless, schooling is — and is publically perceived to be — a vital symbol of social purpose which affects profoundly the beliefs, culture and language of tomorrow's adults. Schooling, and the arrangements we make for it, are a social crucible in which our ideas of social justice and purpose are tried and forged. How well schooling serves our evolving vision of social purpose is related to the nature of that purpose, to a complex, rapidly changing social environment, and, not least, to the arrangements we establish for schooling itself. Schooling and social purpose interact with each other in a complex and endless cycle of purpose, meaning, interpretation and action, a sort of hermeneutic cycle of social policy.[1]

The publicness or privateness of schooling arrangements — or for that matter, arrangements for any mixed or public good — are far from transparently obvious givens. They depend on the combination of funding, provision and governance under which what we call public schools on the one hand and private schools on the other, operate. Certain combinations of funding, provision and regulation are virtually unthinkable within the broad framework of social purpose associated with democracy. Others are unlikely because they lean too far in the direction of one particular social purpose ideology and consequently become politically unacceptable to groups in society whose cooperation is essential if schools as we know them are to exist. Ideologically extreme options, for example a completely de-regulated and privatized schooling arena, are therefore as unlikely to gain political acceptance as ideologically bizarre options such as an unregulated state monopoly.

Nonetheless, the range of funding, provision and governance

combinations seriously considered or actually being tested by governments is clearly broadening as peoples and nations ponder seriously
who and what they are becoming and how schools serve or hinder
their social goals. Combinations that would have been politically
unthinkable two decades ago are now being studied, tolerated and
legislated. This openness to alternative schooling arrangements is
intimately related to demographic change and to changes in the way
we live and work. It is also closely related to a perceived failure of
equalitarian social policy, including universal, compulsory education,
to deliver on its dual promise of excellence and equity.

If, as nations and peoples, we are no longer who we once were,
if, for the most part, we no longer earn our living in anything like the
old ways, why shouldn't our schools both reflect and purposefully
encourage the positive aspects of such social change — both in what
they teach and how they are organized? Have we, in the last analysis,
any choice in the matter? As we become pluralistic communities of
communities rather than culturally homogeneous nation-states, can
schooling models based largely on cultural homogeneity and value
consensus long endure? If they cannot, how can we best conserve and
construct whatever is necessary for social cohesion and economic
productivity? These questions have no easy answers but they are, and
will continue to be, at the heart of discussion about what kind of
arrangements we should allow and encourage for the schooling of
both our young and our not-so-young.

The greatest single temptation confronting governments with
regard to education at the moment may well be to focus too narrowly
on the economic rationale for public education. Yet, in a world where
so many national societies have become radically pluralistic and where
evidence mounts that assimilationist, one-common-curriculum-for-
all approaches to schooling leave many minorities excluded from
educational success and from a place in the social and economic life
of their host societies, a temptation exists to return education to
the home and community, to accept and endorse a rather complete
balkanization of schooling along lines of culture and language. Further
more, given ageing populations and consequent strong and increasing
demands on public resources for health care in many technologically
developed countries, governments are increasingly tempted to say, in
fairly strong policy terms, let us determine what education needs to
be encouraged for economic competitiveness in a high-tech world
market and let us encourage it. For the rest, let people do as they wish
and feel they can afford.

The missing agenda in such reasoning is the ultimate social cost of abandoning completely the ideal of the common school, a shared set of learnings and values for most members of society. If the job market of the future will be a combination of Mcjobs (deskilled work) for the many, and high-tech and senior administration for the few, with not much middle ground between, what *economic* justification can there be for large-scale public investment in skills and knowledge that will, for the most part, remain unused in the marketplace? This way, after all, lies a world of ever-escalating credentialism in which those not able and willing to go the full educational mile are no better off for having gone half the distance. If the economic rationale for education dominates or supplants larger social purpose rationales, quality for the few, rather than access for the many, must define the more essential mission of future government sponsored or encouraged education, at least in the developed nations (and perhaps shortly in the underdeveloped ones as well).[2]

Yet the larger issues of social and biological survival should not be set aside in an enthusiatic rush for high-tech competitiveness and an escape from the evils of government entanglement in the delivery of mixed goods such as schooling — not, at least, if we seriously expect to survive. Our ability to live and work harmoniously and pro-ductively together, and our ability to do so without completely under-mining the ecosystem which gives us life, surely these are social and educational purpose goals fundamental to any kind of future we might have. Policies which educationally, socially and economically disenfranchise minorities and whole classes of persons with certain socioeconomic characteristics, are unlikely to be conducive in the long term to either peace or prosperity. Certainly the view that an unfet-tered free-market serves, in education or elsewhere, the greatest good of the greatest number at the same time that it injures the fewest and in the least objectionable ways, is suspect, *at least as suspect as the pro-position that large, state-operated monopolies do so.* A deregulated free-market, Strike argues, has an intrinsic tendency to concentrate resources on high-ability students while an equalitarian system focused on equity tends inevitably to concentrate resources disproportionately on dis-advantaged students (that is, to follow the compensatory rationale).[3]

Rendering more of the educational task to private entrepreneur-ship may be an important way of extending choice and fostering di-versity in schooling — and of combating the most deleterious effects of unfettered monopoly. The risk, however, in moving too far in the direction of deregulation, private provision and private funding, is more than balkanization and decline in social cohesion. Especially where nominally and officially public schools are made heavily dependent on private resources in order to provide even a basic minimum quality education, the risk involves making all schooling reflective of particularistic private interest. Companies that provide glossy, high-tech science materials — or sponsor 'special' projects or even a 'special' teaching position — will expect schools that benefit from such largesse to inculcate attitudes friendly to their specific corporate activities and interests. In this way, a corporation with, say, an atrocious environmental record or other socially offensive skeletons in the closet, could nonetheless project a very favourable image among the young — *even and especially among the young who are most likely to wield power and influence in the future.*

Support for and experimentation with greater private involvement in nominally public education has by no means been isolated to Great Britain and undoubtedly it has much to recommend itself. Among the advantages of such 'cooperation' are a reduction in the isolation of schools from the workplace, and visible political and moral support from business for the education community including public-sector schools.[4] The danger is that such cooperation can all too easily become cooption. Some evidence exists that the private sector has not, at least in overt ways, 'exchanged their collaboration with the public schools for programs and activities that served their narrow self-interest'.[5] Perhaps, however, they would never have to. One could hardly imagine schools biting the hand that feeds them.

In one respect, there may be little new in all of this. If one concedes that the interests of the business community are more often than not well represented in the creation of social policy, especially educational policy, the influence of business at the school- and district-level is merely more direct than an influence filtered through senior levels of government. The private sector, after all, is the engine of capitalist economies, and government at all levels is rightly at pains to keep that engine from faltering. A distinction, however, should be made between private-sector support and direction that is filtered through government and that which involves far less public acountability and scrutiny. On the one hand, the direct linkage of business and schools has some potentially healthy educational consequences (among the most important, better skill, knowledge and attitudinal preparation for work). On the other hand, some judicious monitoring — call it regulation, if you will — of such cooperation seems essential if publicly funded and operated schools are not to become increasingly identified with particularist private interests. As with all regulation, the challenge is to design regulation that protects the public interest without stifling positive private-sector initiatives that can well serve the public good.

So long as universal attendance and some degree of common learning experience and social formation is seen as socially desirable, part of such regulation should involve fairly careful prescription of basic quality education and policies to ensure reasonable equality of access to it. In short, unless a society is prepared to move far indeed along the conservative social policy agenda road, it will require continual vigilance, and considerable regulatory cost, to prevent governments from surreptitiously transferring an important part of the substantive cost of a basic quality education directly to the private sector under the guise of encouraging school–business cooperation. The temptation to do so is obviously strong where other competing areas of social policy (e.g., health care) have a heavy political imperative behind them. The obvious losers in such a process of surreptitious cost transfer to the private-sector are schools that, for one reason or another, cannot attract private money and resources — or more accurately, the students who attend such schools.

As in all other areas of educational policy, the question of private support inevitably throws one back on the question of what, if any, common, educational experience is necessary and desirable. More fundamentally, we are left to struggle with definitions of educational equity which must inevitably be rooted as much in our assumptions about social purpose and schooling effects as in any empirical evidence. In newly pluralistic and multicultural societies, the challenge of defining educational equity has become a great deal more difficult than it was (or, at least, than it was assumed to be) in the past. We can no longer, for instance, assume that the 'same' curriculum delivered in the same way constitutes equal educational opportunity for majority and minority students. Despite renewed efforts of educational conservatives across the Western world to reassert the common curriculum imperative in relatively ethnocentric and assimilationist terms, too much evidence currently exists that educational policy rooted in commitment to an ideal of identical educational experiences for all, produces extremely unequal educational opportunity and life chances for particular groups in society. Perhaps the greatest irony of such an approach to educational planning is that sameness of instruction ensures that minority students and those from educationally disadvantaged backgrounds will experience in their schools and classes something very different indeed from what middle-class majoritarian children will experience in theirs. The effort to enforce sameness can result in, or at least embrace, the differences we see in some regions between the best public suburban schools and the most lamentably dysfunctional inner-city schools.

Yet the need for some considerable degree of shared basic skills, knowledge, common values and mutual respect is vital if we are to live, work and interact humanely and productively (all in the broadest sense). The delicate balancing of minority content and values suggested in Chapter 8 is an assured agenda item in ongoing debate over social and educational policy for many years to come in newly pluralistic societies seeking to realize the benefits of cultural plurality but avoid the potential for socially apocalyptic fragmentation.

The challenge of the future, in education as in all areas of social policy, is to stake out workable middle-ground solutions to the complex social purpose problems and dilemmas which confront us, and to do so without being bound too rigidly to the structures, patterns and arrangements of the past. Inevitably these solutions will be tentative and evolutionary, but they will be nonetheless important for that fact, since the quality of life our children experience is intimately and inextricably related to the quality of the solutions we devise. In the end, we are most likely to wind up with middle-ground arrangements because ideologically extreme solutions are unlikely to be politically sustainable. Such an outcome, mainly middle-ground solutions in the provision, funding and regulation of education, would be fortuitous because middle-ground solutions are also most likely to assure some modicum of *both* justice and efficiency in the provision of schooling.[6]

For the most part, then, we look to futures in which the preeminence of public education — and the nature of its mission — will be much more actively and comprehensively challenged and debated. Those challenges will be addressed both to its learning and socialization goals on the one hand, and to its structure and funding on the other. More experimentation with privatization in all its guises can be expected — as can more attempts to provide some semblance of choice and competition within publicly funded and operated schooling. Exploration of the limits of the ability of educational vouchers and tax-credits to enlarge access to private schools without undermining their privateness can be expected in more countries and regions.

The range of experimentation with privatization and deregulation, however, will be limited by fears of fatally undermining publicly provided education and thus leaving students in remote or educationally disadvantaged areas prey to the worst effects of an educationally deregulated marketplace — ultimately to loosing all access whatsoever to schooling in areas where private-school entrepreneurs would simply not choose to locate.

Surely any humane vision of a common future must take note of the diversity in our midst; to some extent nurture and celebrate it rather than deny and suppress it. If schooling is a sort of secular, social sacrament, a key social policy instrument which helps to bring about in society what it symbolizes, then it must embrace cultural and linguistic diversity rather than repress it. Cohesive diversity rather than cultural and linguistic homogeneity may be our best social insurance policy, and schools should help write it. The perceived future success or failure, and hence survival, of publicly operated and funded schooling with a universal mandate will almost certainly hinge on its ability to embrace diversity and at the same time ensure some degree of equity in educational results. Just what that equity will mean must be negotiated in each jurisdiction through the political process. What seems certain, however, is that the private schooling option will impact with increasing force on our vision of educational equity and weigh heavily in decisions about what we will allow and what we will mandate in the schooling arena.

No longer can defenders of the public schooling faith feel free to launch frontal assaults on private education. Not only is it evident that such assaults will not rid them of private school competition, direct attacks on private schooling by public school officials inevitably contribute to public suspicion of the motives and mission of public-sector schools. They also undermine the possibility of mutually useful cooperation between public and private-sector schools. Increasingly, advocates of publicly operated schooling will be required to demonstrate to critical, informed, pluralistic and articulate political masters whether, and how, publicly operated schools can better serve the public good — the good of *all* members of the public — than private schools. The mentors and masters of public education will increasingly be forced to accept, work within and recognize the challenge of independent schooling, even private schooling with relatively high levels of public funding. At the end of the day, public schools will not justify their continuance by decrying competition from private, or less public, schools but by meeting the private-school challenge of choice and quality. They must do so, however, within the realities of a radically changed social context, not within the assumptions of traditional ethnocentric, assimilationist logics for educational policy.

Whatever else it may be in the waning decade of the twentieth century, educational policy-making will be neither simple nor comfortable. While many will look upon the changing educational policy field with fear and regret, a real and fundamentally exciting possibility exists of arriving at arrangements that provide better choice, more diversity, and higher quality for many — ideally for most — young and adult learners. The courage to change should, however, be tempered with the vigilance required to maintain and enhance the social benefits of more diffused educational access and opportunity which is at the core of the equalitarian social purpose agenda. Nonetheless, the grand social policy compromises necessary in a pluralistic future should create schooling arenas in which meaningful choice is available to more students than in the past.

Above all, we should vigorously resist a social purpose reductionism which views education *solely* in terms of contribution to economic productivity, of what Strike calls a purely utilitarian focus of distribution in education.[7] The danger of creating societies with an immense social and economic chasm between the many and the few has probably never been greater. Should public support for education come to be based more-or-less exclusively on potential contribution to economic productivity in a high-tech/basic-service-industry economy, we may well rationalize education economically at the expense of fundamental social stability, a pyrrhic victory at best. On the other hand, it is clearly economic performance which ultimately pays the bill for education in any possible funding and governance arrangement. Schooling which neglects its relationship with the work world is a one-way ticket to Third World status.

Everywhere, then, social policy and schooling policy will continue to be, as it always is, a delicate balancing — a careful articulation — of competing values and policy issues. Given the failures and weaknesses of past policy nostrums, the challenge before us at the threshold of the twenty-first century is fourfold. Public policy should foster schooling arenas which avoid the worst mistakes of the past; avail themselves of the potential of education to contribute to the common good in pluralistic societies; and, at the same time, secure social cohesion even as they increase educational equity. What seems abundantly clear is that the future will bring considerable and diverse experimentation in pursuit of such goals.

Notes

1 See page ix.
2 See discussion of labour and educational investment in third-world countries on p. 34.

3   Kenneth Strike, 'The ethics of resource allocation in education: Questions of democracy and justice', in *Microlevel School Finance: Issues and Implications for Policy*, ed. David H. Monk and Julie Underwood (Cambridge, Mass.: Ballinger Publishing Company, 1988), p. 143.

4   Milbrey W. McLaughlin, 'Business and the public schools: New patterns of support', in *Microlevel School Finance: Issues and Implications for Policy*, ed. David H. Monk and Julie Underwood (Cambridge, Mass.: Ballinger Publishing Company, 1988), pp. 74–5.

5   *Ibid.*, p. 72.

6   See p. 59.

7   Strike, 'The ethics of resource allocation', *op cit.*, p. 175.

Bibliography

ADLER, M.J. (1982) *The Paideia Proposal: An Educational Manifesto*, New York, Macmillan, pp. 15–36, 41–5.

ALDRICH, R. (1988a) 'The national curriculum: An historical perspective', in LAWTON, D. and CHITTY, C. (Eds) *The National Curriculum*, London, Billing and Way, pp. 22–3.

ALDRICH, R. (1988b) 'The national curriculum debate in England: An historical perspective' paper presented October 27, 1988 at the Faculty of Education, The University of Western Ontario, London, Ontario.

ALEXANDER, K. and PALLAS, A. (1983) 'Private schools and public policy: New evidence on cognitive achievement in public and private schools', *Sociology of Education*, 56, October, pp. 170–82.

ALEXANDER, K. and PALLAS, A. (1984) 'In defense of "private schools and public policy": Reply to Kilgore', *Sociology of Education*, 57, 1, January, pp. 56–8.

ANDERSON, R.D. (1983) 'Education and the state in nineteenth-century Scotland', *The Economic History Review*, 2nd Series, 36, 4, November, pp. 518–34.

ANTHONY, P. (1987) 'Public monies for private schools: The Supreme Court's changing approach', *Journal of Education Finance*, 12, 4, Spring, pp. 592–605.

ATKINSON, R. (1986) *Government Against the People: The Economics of Political Exploitation*, Southampton, The Camelot Press, pp. 46–57.

BARMAN, J. (1984) *Growing up British in British Columbia: Boys in Private School*, Vancouver, University of British Columbia Press, p. 79.

BENSON, C. (1968) *The Economics of Public Education*, 2nd ed., Boston, Houghton Mifflin, p. 131.

BERGEN, J. (1981) 'The private school movement in Canada', *Education Canada*, 21, June, p. 8.

BERGEN, J. (1986) 'Choice in schooling', *Journal of Educational Administration and Foundations*, 1, 1, June, pp. 40, 46–7.

BERNSTEIN, B. (1971) *Class, Codes and Control*, London, Routledge & Kegan Paul, 1, pp. 170–87.

BLOOM, A. (1987) *The Closing of the American Mind*, New York, Simon and Schuster.

BLUM, V. (1981) 'Why inner-city families send their children to private schools: An empirical study', in GAFFNEY, E.M. (Ed.) *Private Schools and the Public Good: Policy Alternatives for the Eighties*, Notre Dame, University of Notre Dame Press, pp. 17–24.

BOURDIEU, P. and PASSERON, J.C. (1977) *Reproduction in Education, Society and Culture*, NICE, R. (trans) London, Sage Publications, pp. 3–68.

BRIMELOW, P. (1984) 'Public and private schools: The need for competition', *Education Digest*, 49, 8, April, pp. 14–17.

BRUNER, J. (1963) *The Process of Education*, Toronto, Vintage Books, pp. 33–54.

BURT, W. (1981) 'The new campaign for tax credits: "Parachiaid" misses the point', in MANLEY-CASIMIR, M. (Ed.) *Family Choice in Schooling*, Toronto, D.C. Heath and Company, pp. 154, 157, 165.

CAIN, G. and GOLDBERGER, A. (1983) 'Public and private schools revisited', *Sociology of Education*, 56, 4, October, pp. 208–18.

CANTOR, L. (1987) 'The role of the private sector in vocational education and training: The case of Japan's special training schools', *The Vocational Aspect of Education*, 39, 103, August, pp. 35–41.

CHITTY, C. (1988) 'Two models of a national curriculum: Origins and interpretation', in LAWTON, D. and CHITTY, C. (Eds) *The National Curriculum*, London, Billing and Way, pp. 34–48.

CHITTY, C. (1989) *Towards a New Education System: The Victory of the New Right?* London, Falmer Press, pp. 106–28, 197, 212–15, 218, 220, 223.

CHURCHILL, S. (1986) *The Education of Linguistic and Cultural Minorities in the OECD Countries*, Clevedon, Multilingual Matters Ltd., pp. 33–60, 54–6, 114–62.

COLEMAN, J.S. *et al.* (1966) *Equality of Educational Opportunity*, Washington, DC, U.S. Department of Health, Education and Welfare, p. 22.

COOKSON, P. JR. (1982) 'Boarding schools and the moral community', *The Journal of Educational Thought*, 16, 2, August, pp. 89–97.

COONS, J. and SUGARMAN, S. (1981) 'Educational tax credits versus school vouchers: Comment on the California tuition tax credit proposal', in MANLEY-CASIMIR, M. (Ed.) *Family Choice in Schooling*, Toronto, D.C. Heath and Company, pp. 169–77.

COOPER, B., MCLAUGHLIN, D. and MANNO, B. (1983) 'The latest word on private school growth', *Teachers College Record*, 85, 1, Fall, pp. 88–98.

DAVIES, L. (1981) 'Alternatives in education from the Third World', in HARBER, C., MEIGHAM, R. and ROBERTS, B. (Eds) *Alternative Educational Futures*, London, Holt, Rinehart and Winston, pp. 63–77.

DEPARTMENT OF EDUCATION AND SCIENCE PRESS RELEASE 343/87 (1987) 'The Education Reform Bill', 20 November, as quoted in WEDELL, K. (1988)

'The National Curriculum and special educational needs', in LAWTON, D. and CHITTY, C. (Eds) *The National Curriculum*, London, Billing and Way, p. 111.

DEWEY, J. (1977) *Education Today*, Westport, Conn., Greenwood, pp. 273–9.

DEWEY, J. (1964) *Democracy and Education*, New York, Macmillan, pp. 69–99.

DOYLE, D. (1981a) 'Public funding and private schooling: The state of descriptive and analytic research', in GAFFNEY, E. (Ed.) *Private Schools and the Public Good: Policy Alternatives for the Eighties*, Notre Dame, University of Notre Dame Press, pp. 71–8.

DOYLE, D. (1981b) 'A din of inequity: Private schools reconsidered', *Teachers College Record*, 82, 4, Summer, pp. 661–73.

DURNIN, M. (1988) 'The new Alberta School Act', *Our Schools, Our Selves*, 1, 1, October, pp. 96–105.

EDMONDS, E.L. (1981) 'In defense of the private schools', *Education Canada*, 21, 3, Fall, pp. 21–3, 48.

EDWARDS, T., FITZ, J. and WHITTY, G. (1985) 'Private schools and public funding: A comparison of recent policies in England and Australia', 21, 1, March, pp. 29–45.

FARRELL, J. (1987) 'Cultural differences and Curriculum Inquiry', *Curriculum Inquiry*, 17, 1, Spring, pp. 1–7.

FINN, C.E. JR. (1981) 'Why public and private schools matter', *Harvard Educational Review*, 51, 4, November, p. 511–14.

FISHER, D. (1981) 'Family choice and education: Privatizing a public good', in MANLEY-CASIMIR, M. (Ed.) *Family Choice in Schooling*, Toronto, D.C. Heath and Company, p. 204.

FRIEDMAN, M. (1962) *Capitalism and Freedom*, Chicago, University of Chicago Press, pp. 12–21.

GAGNON, J. (1986) 'Pour rendre l'excellence accessible', *Prospectives: Revue d'information et de recherche en éducation*, 22, février, p. 23.

GARNER, W. and HANNAWAY, J. (1982) 'Private schools: The client connection', in MANLEY-CASIMIR, M. (Ed.) *Family Choice in Schooling*, Toronto, D.C. Heath and Company, p. 127.

GIROUX, H. (1981) *Ideology, Culture and the Process of Schooling*, Philadelphia, Temple University Press and Falmer Press, pp. 75–112.

GOFFMAN, E. (1961) *Asylums*, Chicago, Aldine Publishing, pp. 3–124.

GOSSAGE, C. (1977) *A Question of Privilege: Canada's Independent Schools*, Toronto, Peter Martin Associates, p. 280.

HALL, P. *et al.* (1975) *Change, Choice, and Conflict in Social Policy*, London, Heinemann, pp. 475–86.

HEYNEMAN, S. (1988) 'A look at the 1990s: Financing education a decade from now in developing countries', paper delivered March 18, 1988, to the Annual Meeting of the American Education Finance Association, Tampa, Florida.

HOGAN, M. (1984) *Public vs. Private Schools: Funding and Directions in Austra-*

lia, Victoria, Penguin Books Australia Limited, pp. 1, 52, 83, 86, 103, 116.

HOLMES, M. (1982) 'Progress or progressive decline? A response to Howard Russel's Review of *Progress in Education* by Nigel Wright', *Curriculum Inquiry*, 12, Winter, pp. 419–32.

HOLT, J. (1981) *Teaching Your Own: A Hopeful Path for Education*, New York, Delacorte Press/Seymour Lawrence Book, p. 231.

ILLICH, I. (1971) *Deschooling Society*, New York, Harper and Row, pp. 9–24, 38–40, 42–4.

JAMES, E. (1984) 'Benefits and costs of privatized public services: Lessons from the Dutch educational system', *Comparative Education Review*, 28, 4, November, pp. 605–24.

JAMES, E. (1987) 'The public/private division of responsibility for education: An international comparison', *Economics of Education Review*, 6, p. 11.

JENCKS, C. (1972) *Inequality: A Reassessment of the Effect of Family and Schooling in America*, Harmondsworth, Penguin, p. 226.

JENSEN, A.R. (1968) 'Biogenetic perspectives: An introduction', in DEUTSCH, M., KATZ, I. and JENSEN, A.R. (Eds) *Social Class, Race, and Psychological Development*, New York, Holt, Rinehart and Winston, p. 9.

JENSEN, A.R. (1973) *Educability and Group Differences*, London, Methuen & Co. Ltd., pp. 243–53, 259.

JOHNSON, D. (1987) *Private Schools and State Systems: Two Systems or One?* Philadelphia, Open University Press, p. 7.

KEARNS, D.T. (1988) 'An education recovery plan for America', *Phi Delta Kappan*, 69, April, p. 566.

KURAIN, G.T. (1988) *Major Countries: Algeria-Hungary, vol. I of World Education Encyclopedia*, New York, Facts on File Publications, pp. 410, 452–4.

LAWTON, D. (1988) 'Ideologies of education', in LAWTON, D. and CHITTY, C. (Eds) *The National Curriculum*, London, Billing and Way, pp. 10–20.

LAWTON, S. (1985) Unpublished report on sectarian schooling arrangements, p. 161.

LEUNG, K. (1984) 'Ethnic schools and public education: A study of the relationship between ethnic schools and public education in Alberta', Masters thesis, University of Calgary.

LINES, P.M. (1986) 'The new private schools and their historic purpose', *Phi Delta Kappan*, 67, 5, January, pp. 373–9.

McLAUGHLIN, M.W. (1988) 'Business and the public schools: New patterns of support', in MONK, D.H. and UNDERWOOD, J. (Eds) *Microlevel School Finance: Issues and Implications for Policy*, Cambridge, Mass., Ballinger Publishing Company, pp. 72, 74–5.

MAW, J. (1988) 'National curriculum policy: Coherence and progression', in LAWTON, D. and CHITTY, C. (Eds) *The National Curriculum*, London, Billing and Way, pp. 56, 58, 60–2.

MERTON, R.K. (1965) *Social Theory and Social Structure*, New York, The Free Press, pp. 225–386.

Moss, P. (1985) 'A response to Mel Shipman', *Orbit*, 16, 2, April, pp. 14–15.

Murphy, J. *Church, State and Schools in Britain, 1800–1970*, London, Routledge & Kegan Paul, p. 125.

Murphy, R. (1987) 'A changing role for examination boards', in Horton, T. (Ed.) *GCSE: Examining the New System*, Cambridge, Harper and Row, pp. 1–11.

Musgrave, R.A. and Musgrave, P.B. (1980) *Public Finance in Theory and Practice*, New York, McGraw-Hill Book Co., pp. 79, 304–5, 318–19.

The National Commission on Excellence in Education (1984) *A Nation At Risk*, Cambridge, Mass., USA Publishing, pp. 5–14, 69–76.

O'Keefe, D. (1987) *The Times Educational Supplement*, 18 September, as quoted in Maw, J. 'National curriculum policy: Coherence and progression', pp. 61–2.

Olivas, M.A. (1981) 'Information inequities: A fatal flaw in parochiaid plans', in Gaffney, E.M. (Ed.) *Private Schools and the Public Good: Policy Alternatives for the Eighties*, Notre Dame, University of Notre Dame Press, p. 138.

Parry, J.P. (1971) *The Provision of Education in England and Wales*, London, George Allen and Unwin Ltd., pp. 88–96.

Paquette, J. (1989a) 'The Quality Conundrum: Assessing what we cannot agree on', in Lawton, S. and Wignall, R. (Eds) *Scrimping or Squandering?: Financing Canadian Schools*, Toronto, OISE Press, pp. 11–28.

Paquette, J. (1989b) 'Minority education policy: Assumptions and propositions', *Curriculum Inquiry*, 19, 4, December, pp. 405–20.

Paquette, J. (1989c) 'From propositions to prescriptions: Belief, power and the problem of minority education', *Curriculum Inquiry*, 19, 4, December, pp. 437–51.

Perrow, C. (1986) *Complex Organizations: A Critical Essay*, 3rd ed., New York, Random House, p. 270.

Perry, N.J. (1988) 'Saving the schools: How business can help', *Fortune*, 118, 11, November, pp. 42–56.

Pring, R. (1987) 'Privatization in education', *Journal of Education Policy*, 2, 4, December, pp. 13, 289–99.

Radwanski, G. (1987) *Ontario Study of the Relevance of Education and the Issue of Dropouts*, Toronto, Ontario Ministry of Education, pp. 25–64.

Rand, A. *Atlas Shrugged*, New York, Random House, p. 663.

Richards, D. and Ratsoy, E. (1987) *Introduction to the Economics of Canadian Education*, Calgary, Detselig Enterprises Ltd., pp. 71–2.

Roszak, T. (1986) *The Cult of Information: The Folklore of Computers and the True Art of Thinking*, New York, Pantheon.

Roy, W. (1987) 'The teacher viewpoint', in Horton, T. (Ed.) *GCSE: Examining the New System*, Cambridge, Harper and Row, pp. 12–17.

Russel, H.H. (1977) 'What progress in education?' Review of Nigel Wright's *Progress in Education*, London, Croom Helm, *Curriculum Inquiry*, 12, 1, Spring, pp. 105–14.

RYAN, D. (1986) *Developing a New Model of Teacher Effectiveness: Lessons Learned from the IEA Classroom Environment Study*, Toronto, Ministry of Education, pp. 1–14.

ST. CLAIR, R. and LEAP, W. (Eds) (1982) *Language Renewal among American Indian Tribes: Issues, Problems and Prospects*, Rosslyn, Virgina, National Clearinghouse for Bilingual Education.

SANDERS, J. (1990) 'From ought to is: Radwanski and the moralistic fallacy', in ALLISON, D. and PAQUETTE, J. (Eds) *Reform and Relevance in Schooling: Dropouts, Destreaming, and the Common Curriculum*, Toronto, OISE Press.

SHARKANSKY, I. (1970) *The Routines of Politics*, New York, Van Nostrand-Reinhold.

SHIPMAN, M. (1985) 'Funding independent schools', *Orbit* 16, 1, February, pp. 8–9.

SHOR, I. (1986) 'Equality is excellence: Transforming teacher education and the learning process', *Harvard Educational Review*, 56, 4, June, pp. 406–26.

SMITH, A. (1961) *An Inquiry into the Nature and Causes of the Wealth of Nations*, MAZLISH, B. (Ed.) New York, Bobbs-Merrill, pp. 55–62.

STRIKE, K. (1988) 'The ethics of resource allocation in education: Questions of democracy and justice', in MONK, D.H. and UNDERWOOD, J. (Eds) *Microlevel School Finance: Issues and Implications for Policy*, Cambridge, Mass., Ballinger Publishing Company, pp. 143, 175.

TANGUAY, V. and GIARD, B. (1985) 'La qualité de l'enseignement ou l'éducation en évolution', *Information*, PAQUETTE, J. (trans) 24, 5, November, p. 41.

TIEBOUT, C.M. (1956) 'A pure theory of local expenditures', *Journal of Political Economy*, 64, 5, October, pp. 416–24.

US DEPARTMENT OF HEALTH, EDUCATION AND WELFARE (1966) *Equality of Educational Opportunity*, COLEMAN et al., (Eds) Washington.

WALFORD, G. (1987) 'How dependent is the independent sector?' *Oxford Review of Education*, 13, 3, October, pp. 275–96.

WARNOCK, M. (1988) *A Common Policy for Education*, Oxford, Oxford University Press, p. 173, as quoted in CHITTY, *Towards a New Education System: The Victory of the New Right*, p. 197.

WEDELL, K. (1988) 'The national curriculum and special educational needs', in LAWTON, D. and CHITTY, C. (Eds) *The National Curriculum*, London, Billing and Way, p. 111.

WEST, E. (1981) 'The public monopoly and the seeds of self-destruction', in MANLEY-CASIMIR, M. (Ed.) *Family Choice in Schooling*, Toronto, D.C. Heath and Company, pp. 185–98.

Index